EPICS 3:
POEMS #29-#43
BY S. E. MCKENZIE

Copyright © 2015 S. E. McKenzie
All rights reserved.
ISBN-13: 978-1772810028

ISBN-10: 1772810029

DEDICATION
To everyone who has been left out in the cold

THIS BOOK IS A BOOK OF SPECULATIVE FICTION. Characters, companies, governments, places, events, are either products of the author's imagination or used fictitiously. Any resemblance to persons (living or dead), companies, governments, places and/or events, is a coincidence.

CONTENTS

THIS BOOK IS A BOOK OF SPECULATIVE FICTION. iv

CONTENTS 1

#29. STUCK ON THE WHEEL 3

#30. UNDERCLASS 35

#31. THE PROGRAM 46

#32. DEATH PANEL 59

#33. BIGGIE 80

#34. SPINning 105

#35. REbeat 148

#36. REBOUND: If you can 169

#37. FRAMED 192

#38. LIGHT 205

#39. CHAOS 220

#40. PULSE 228

#41. THE DENOMINATOR 244

#42. THE PULL 253

#43. CRACKER 263

S.E. McKENZIE

STUCK ON THE WHEEL

#29. STUCK ON THE WHEEL

I

Life is round
A true circle;
A cycle

Crashes
When pedaling
Stops.

Cycles;
Boom
And bust,

Left over treasure
Piled up
To rust.

Were we born
Just to die
And turn into dust?

We carry paper
Which says
'In God we Trust."

II

What is more ruthless?
Laws of Nature
Or Military Man?

What is more truthless? Hell;
Boots marching on the ground;
Blowing up bridges all around;

As town after town
Has life
Turning upside down.

Callous and hardened
From many years of war
Frame of mind has turned unkind.

To occupy one must be willfully blind.
To live and let die
Without shedding a tear;

The occupied were immersed in all their fear.
As town after town
Destroyed themselves;

EPICS 3

While the occupiers were marching near.

Stopped to stand on the hill,
And watched neighbor
Kill neighbor;

No longer a stranger's prisoner.
They only saw danger
In each other;

So willing to kill
Sister and brother;
So willing to kill

One another.

Before they died
At their enemy's hand;
And have their land

And home disappear;
Leaving them with no hope
Just degradation and fear.

S.E. McKENZIE

III
Hell?
Ghosts roaming the earth
Without being able to touch or taste

All that they love;
Not yet ready to die;
Their souls could not fly

To the heavens above.

And beneath;

The scariest world of all
Is a world without Love,
Or compassion.

Being looked through
As if your mind
Was not there.

Abuse of discretionary power
Dissolving another's content
Without a care.

EPICS 3

Manufacturing
Consent
As if a person's was not there.

IV

We never were defeated
Even though the other side
Told us that we would be better off

If we were deleted.

We would not commit suicide;
Even though what we were clinging to
Was being threatened by the enemy's acts.

The foreign police
Differentiated us;
They bigotized us;

They criticized us.
They screamed at us
To stop.

S.E. McKENZIE

If we had
We would have
Been defeated.

We took a stand,
Never to be deleted.
We held each other's hand

And stood tall;
In the Negative Zone
Many were pushed

Into the fall;
So alone
Forever unequal;

The privileged
Felt so gleeful;
Marching boots

Echoed through the land.
We took each other's hand;
As they undervalued us;

EPICS 3

They said
There was only one escape
For us;

The barriers went up;
As the foreign elite filled their cup;
They said our time was up.

And I knew being so unequal
Was stifling
Me and you;

What a deal for them;
What a steal;
Leaving us to beg for our next meal;

After working overtime
We all knew the crime;
And the enemy force was frightening;

The gap was widening;
Even though our spinning world
Revolved around one sun;

S.E. McKENZIE

While the new Gestapo
Replaced
The old Gestapo.

Today, we don't think twice
We know when to run;
Nouveau Gestapo

Can't control his gun.

The idle rich accuse and abuse
All day long;
They fear that the poor

Will take over their yard.
Nouveau Gestapo stays on guard;
Plays the host;

For the library is his post;
He hears complaints day after day
That poor looking people are sitting in chairs

And are in the way;

EPICS 3

Still clinging to the truth
Now only found
In holy books;

So dusty; along library walls;
Old society lost;
Occupiers never knew the cost;

Nouveau Gestapo
Replaced the Old Gestapo;
Too afraid of risk

To let go;
Still clinging
To books now on fire;

Nouveau Gestapo waved the poor away;
Never to be the same
Again;

For what was broken inside
Kept most afraid of the unknown.
As their chains were taken away;

S.E. McKENZIE

They were too afraid to run;
So they stayed;
While the enemy displayed

Their weapons of war
On parade
Rewards of aggression.

They never spoke in words
We could understand;
They only spoke of oppression.

We were now under their command;
As they idled in lots
After killing every tree.

They were the Avant Guard
Of the new Parasite
Society.

Noxious fumes spread into a place called Infinity.
The air was harder to breathe;
We were now victims of their regression;

EPICS 3

Why no one cried
When they died
We will never know;

The enemy loved
Their false ego
So its projection lived on.

We know how Nouveau Gestapo lies.
And if it wasn't for the sun
The world would be as cold

As gold;
While Unethical Legalist
Enjoyed the pain

He created for some
Mostly young;
Some went insane;

Self-fulfilling prophecy
Like the end of the world
Where common sense

S.E. McKENZIE

Was no longer allowed.
Silently the people
Lost themselves into the crowd.

And only the birds were allowed to be free.

For Heaven had closed its door
And we were left more alone
Than we ever before.

It was hard to cope;
A stranger offered dope;
The Nouveau Gestapo's rope.

And so many had been

Bigotized;
Personal content
Wiped off the slate;

Now they were victim
Of mass hate;
They had to smile sweetly

EPICS 3

To avoid a grizzly fate.

We avoided crashing onto the ground.
So we continued
Unbroken;

Our power
Was in self-knowledge
And that knowledge had awoken;

Our unified voice had spoken.

We were now as one;
And the collective soul
Would never die;

It lives and sleeps up in the sky.
Though we know the foe
By name;

Our motivation
Was more than just a game;
To us;

And how they laughed
As they watched us everyday;
Wishing that we would go away.

S.E. McKENZIE

The barriers went up
One by one;
Then we knew

The processing had begun.

The rules
Written by militarized fools
Kept so many divided;

Kept power lopsided;
What was important
Was left undecided;

Opposite poles
Had collided;
While we refused to be misguided;

The pull of attraction was building;
And we would not be defeated;
We had no right to life;

Even though we refused to be deleted.

V
Time
Went on
Without a clock

EPICS 3

But when an opportunity
Was about to knock
We had to have a door;

A place to call our own;
A home;
A place to rest our heads.

And we were bigotized;
Just like before
We refused to be deleted;

The enemy told us to stop;
But if we had
We would have been defeated.

So we held on to our dream;

Did not respond to their scream;
Even though they said they were in control;
Chaos was their ruthless boss;

For true life was round
And had to spin.
The most privileged

S.E. McKENZIE

Had very thin skin;
And were so easy to offend;
By anyone they did not invite;

They flexed their might
To spite
Those they knew would lose a fight.

And the clique of sheik
Agreed
Anyone in need

Must not be seen
For the prosperity of the town
Would be questioned

Bringing property values down.
And the Clique of sheik
Had a hard line

Even though true life was always round
So the world could spin
Around one sun;

EPICS 3

The wise knew how to bend
With the curve
Gave the Collective Soul

A one percent chance to mend.

Though having hard lines
Saved time
We knew their crime.

And kept the circle turning
For True Life was round
And there was no way out

Accept one;
We never lost Hope;
We said no to their dope;

Gestapo's rope;
For our world
Turned around One Sun.

And we were young; our life had just begun;
They said it was best for us
To be deleted

S.E. McKENZIE

But we disagreed
We tried to find a way
To be freed;

We fought for our collective life;
Refused to be defeated
We kept our perspective; for we were fed

From the love above;
And the light of the sun
Gave us the energy to run;

From Big Brother who did not know

What He had done;
For the Prison State of Hate
Would determine Fate,

If Love did not grow
Before it was
Too late.

We refused to be defeated;
And we refused to be deleted;
For we were young; and our life had just begun.

EPICS 3

Though we walked in pain
We knew we had
So much to gain

We knew;
What could not be sustained
Would self-destruct;

And equity lost
Would be the cost
For the city

With little day time economy;
And depended on the Economy of the Night
Filled with Neon Light.

Beer, guns and short term profit
Led many astray;
So stereotyped in Neon Hype;

We turned away;

So we could build synergy;
Generating energy
Before the time

S.E. McKENZIE

Was gone.
Without a system to integrate
Social order would disintegrate.

Social disorder was the only growth industry
In the two block town;
We watched them march all around;

Pushing the most vulnerable
To the ground.
Social policy was written

"Don't let them stay around";

And then after the most vulnerable went missing
A new policy was written
By the same policy makers;

"A study has to be done
To determine why the missing were missing;"
And then the unwritten words were said;

"If the missing were found
Beat them into the ground
And turn their world upside down

EPICS 3

So they will go missing again,
Cause we don't want them around,
So beat them into the ground."

And the truth
Would be spun
Inside Alien Nation"

By the same policy makers;

Common sense
Was not allowed;
We were better off

Lost in the crowd.

Wearing a frown
And a cross around their neck
They were in heaven

When they gave us heck.
The missing were now in the ground
Never to be found;

Social justice Policy
Never written
But understood

S.E. McKENZIE

By the Gestapo in the Hood;
Desensitized
He never knew why

He turned a blind eye
While the young
Were turned away

Said they fell through the cracks;
Like they do every day;
Nouveau Gestapo turned a blind eye too;

Left the young to die
Hidden; within History;
Repeated Misery;

The old men
Died their hair
And went out to dance;

Before they fell asleep;
For evermore
Resting in Infinity's Tomb

EPICS 3

Where there is always room
For the next generation
When their time has come.

Today; only the birds were free to be.

VI

Time had come and gone
Leaving us older;
Amongst new young;

Patterns of design;
If you know them
You will know your own mind.

Social Inclusion
Did not pay
For the few growth industries

Were now Social Disorder
And Global War;
Scariest World of all

Is a world without Love.

S.E. McKENZIE

VII

Revolving door;
Push and shove;
Into a blue world without Love.

Love refused to die;
Or be broken;
And Love was in despair;

Love was never meant
To live in a world
Where so few would dare to care;

Never brave enough
To open
Their hearts

To Love;
Even though
No one

Wanted to live
In a world
Without Love.

EPICS 3

VIII

We did not know if the sun would decay
In some hidden way;
The sun gave life;

And the sun
Shined;
In and around new life

So noble and pure;

Without the sun
Life would freeze
And Transform into death;

Frozen breath;
And no longer be
Alive or free.

To kiss you and me.

The sun held Earth
In position
While Earth

Rotated without division;
Why ask why?
It is always that way;

S.E. McKENZIE

The effect of the sun
On everything on earth
Was a feeding cycle;

Growing the food chain
Which tied us
Together as one.

But why worry about such things?

IV

What will we repair,
In this time of despair?
Wealth accumulates;

Food Chain Politics
Run by dicks
Taking selfie-pics

Hidden in pockets;
Rockets; shape our borders
Through destruction;

Moving in a direction
We never chose;
Social ord

EPICS 3

Has declined;
Differential treatment
To break your mind;

Differential treatment
Based on
How one was defined;

Social Disorder;
Growth industry;
See the benefactors

Rushing through the isle
In the grocery store
Without a smile;

Push and shove
In a world without love;
Fake apology

While you are left
Spread eagle on the floor
Just like the night before.

S.E. McKENZIE

As they push you out of the way.
New social order
Threatening to close every border;

How they complain;
They expected more gain;
When they turned a blind eye

To their neighbor's pain;
So willfully blind;
They made the world less kind.

Mean girls sitting on shelves
Behind the steely watchers
Hiding their guns;

Think about it too long
It will give you the runs;
Don't let what they have done

Linger in your mind;
For your armor will protect you
For ever more;

EPICS 3

Don't close your mind
Just close your door
And your eyes too;

For only the birds
Were really
Free to be

We had no time to reflect;
Had suffered years of neglect;
Would never be a member of the select;

Those who the system would protect;
Thin skinned;
Quick to differentiate

Between the haves and have nots;
Quick to take offence
Would treat the have-nots as worthy

Of less than two cents.

You would never be
A member of the select few;
That was true;

That is why
I love you;
I thought you knew.

For True Life
Was round;
For Spin's sake

Don't get lost
In their hard line;
Used to define

The unborn
And those
Life has torn

Now living in Infinity
For evermore
For Heaven has closed its door.

X
Hungry Bear
Caught in Apple Tree;
Bear knew it was the end.

EPICS 3

The bullet pierced his heart
And ours too
As the mighty beast

Whimpered before he died.

XI
Concrete jungle
Would never show from below;
But when we flew above
We saw so little Love.

THE END

S.E. McKENZIE

UNDERCLASS

#30. UNDERCLASS
I

Personal Space; Saving Grace;
Opportunity to reach potential;
Where positive direction is essential.

Stuck under the overpass,
They say they hate
Her Face;

Without make-up;
Nouveau Gestapo made up;
After he was paid up.

Question this circle?
Why would they?
They count their cash

Every Pay Day.
"We fight for dignity,"
He said

"We don't fight back"
He said.
"Non-Violence fills them with dread,"

S.E. McKENZIE

He said.
We will be more than a colony
In waiting.

Nouveau Gestapo said;
"Though I was busy dating;
The bait is set;

We will grow a penal colony
Over your head;
We will stay supreme

Until you scream
Somewhere all alone;
Until you submit;

Until you atone."

II

Never had a car;
Don't have a telephone;
We live under the overpass;

We live there all alone;

EPICS 3

We awake with our hearts pounding;
For the surrounding beauty
Is astounding.

We are on the move
When the mob
Scares us to bits;

They ask the girls to show their…

We sit in the Library
Hoping for relaxation
Sharing a bit of civilization.

Nouveau Gestapo
Is on his beat
Tells us to get back onto our feet;

Out of cash; we are the new underclass;
Never bought gas
Now we must go back

To the overpass.

S.E. McKENZIE

We are just the residential underclass
Hoping for peace of mind
Never reaching our potential

We will never be loved
We are inconsequential;
Looking for someone kind

In a dead end town of the willfully blind.

II

There was no clue,
Or so they said,
When they found her severed head.

The shock was great;
Filled us with hate;
First responders were there too late.

The passers-by said they had no phone;
We didn't believe them
We felt so alone.

The passers-by looked at me
Then looked away;
There was nothing they would say;

EPICS 3

Though now I know; the rumor
That framed me;
Began that way;

And no one could bring Emilee

Back to me.
For Emilee
Was now free

Though I never would be.

No longer a member
Of the residential underclass;
No longer stuck under the overpass

Now I was in cage for the rest of my days.

III

No one heard her scream
But me;
For I was hiding.

I had no phone; I was all alone;
And I could not see.
I was frozen in fear

S.E. McKENZIE

Though I could hear
Heavy footsteps
Above my head.

After the final scream
I knew Emilee was dead.
And that was the time

When something
Inside me
Had broken open;

To a new force
Which had just awoken.
As rumors were spun

I was also a victim of what he had done.

IV
First responders Jethro and Bill
Were having a barbecue
With a senator on the hill.

They only came by
To do their job;
Write out a form;

EPICS 3

And do the norm;
Bill threw a flower
On the wooden box

Where Emilee lay;
There was not much to say;
Though her memory

Would never fade away;
Even to this day
I see the haunted look

Left on Emilee's severed face.

V

Though Jethro and Bill were very late
They offered no explanation
For we were the last

Of the forgotten generation;
Senator Puffy
Stayed on the hill;

While Jethro and Bill
Pondered the meaning
Of every invoice

S.E. McKENZIE

They had to see
Before they examined Emilee;
Then they asked me

If I knew who the suspect was;
For Emilee had no voice
Never had a choice

Before she lost her life
On that fateful night
Under the overpass.

Jethro and Bill
Said that the suspect
Was me.

They asked me why
I didn't respond
Since I was there;

They asked me why I didn't care;
They threw projection after projection
At me until I wanted to scream;

EPICS 3

For I was a residential underclass;
In a system now old and demented;
They knew I had never consented

To have everything I said
Used against me
Until the day I was dead.

Jethro and Bill
Demonized,
Marginalized,

And then socialized
With the senator on the hill
Who was shredding

Invoice after invoice;
It sounded like a thrill.
Jethro and Bill

Turned my world upside down;
The glass ceiling is now the floor;
Never had a chance;

Just like before.

And to this day
I have not been free;
For the deeds of that night

Done by someone who wasn't me;
Jethro and Bill
Always asked who else could it be?

In less than an hour I was processed
And doomed;
While Emilee's killer

Roamed free

Waiting
To pounce
Under the overpass;

Where everything is out of sight.
If you get too close
You won't survive the night.

THE END

THE PROGRAM

#31. THE PROGRAM
I

Whisper, whisper, whisper;
With deadly force;
Whisper, whisper, whisper;

In a shrinking world.

The liquidator
The contractor
The phony negotiator.

Whisper, whisper, whisper;
Trip em up
So we can watch

Rip em up;
By Quasi Developer-Lord;
Tearing down outside wall.

Inside was home; so very small;
While the other side
Was tattered and torn.

In a shrinking world.

EPICS 3

Continual gong show;
In la la land;
Lost the connection;

Ear phones were plugged in;
Now you have a digital wall;
For people to climb around;

Knock down;
So they don't feel so small;
In a shrinking world.

II

Do not get crushed in the rush;
For the world is not flat
And the roundness

Makes what you give
Come back
In a new form;

With a tireless drive
To survive
In the divided; shrinking world.

S.E. McKENZIE

Communication channels
Sometimes undervalued;
Sometimes overvalued;

Rarely understood;
How they shrink
The world around us.

While many fall on their face
With cameras all over the place,
The hardness grew.

In a shrinking world;
Whisper, whisper, whisper;
Nosy neighbor

Filled your bin with newspaper;

You get the fine
You get defined;
Whisper, whisper, whisper,

EPICS 3

The smell of adult onset,
Is all around;
Filed on the Internet.

Whisper, whisper, whisper.

Not just any legal mafia; they own your sister.
Ego Clash, skin flash;
Everyone wants to be the man.

Whisper, whisper, whisper;
We have a deal for you.
Open economy

Until the barrier is installed;
To beautify your block;
Nouveau Gestapo declares;

No shock; the world is unfair.

Shrinking world
At your door;
Stuff is in demand

S.E. McKENZIE

More than ever before.

Whisper, whisper, whisper.
The liquidator;
The contractor,

The phony negotiator.
Rumor; maker; make-believe science;
Lost connection;

After they strangled you in debt;
The barrier to beautify
Glowed and gloated.

III
Soon one side
Was more bloated than the other side;
The new tyranny.

One side spends money
From the other side
Building the future

For the other side.
Inside
Shrinking world inflates false pride.

EPICS 3

Outside; one side
Will tear it all down;
People wanting a new life,

A dime a dozen;
Lying to each other;
Killing sister and brother;

Neighbor feuding with neighbor.
Blame the poorest of all
For the fall.

In this shrinking world.

IV
Global warming;
Coast to coast
Love was still the force

Which mattered the most.
Cost; Paradise lost;
State

Adds to collapse;
Steely faced
Creating the underclass;

S.E. McKENZIE

Foreclosure of the overpass.

One side;
What a wonderful world;
The other side

Lost in the war.
In the forever
Shrinking world.

V

Fuel for negativity,
War on drugs.
Discrimination and lack of objectivity.

An excuse for the Fear Monger;
IT propagandist; to sell more
Government endorsed drug;

Alcohol;
Gap is natural; part of our agenda;
They say;

Takes so much time; we need overpay.

EPICS 3

Whisper, whisper, whisper;
Secret society projects agenda;
Money driven segregation;

Knocks you down.

Shrinking world
Owned by a few;
Dehumanized by greed

Stigmatized by need;
With no reflection;
Too easy to strike back.

When no one sheds a tear
For your innocence lost
Knows no opportunity cost.

While looking at you with fear
Creates a feeling
That reflects; projects;

Negative energy
Of illusion
Whatever you think or feel

Will be called delusion.
If you don't kneel to the carrot-stick god;
You could lose your way in confusion.

VI

What a night to remember
A night of purpose
A night of contradiction.

Fate,
A prison state;
That cannot change.

Said the steely faced
Gun totting
One industry town man;

Only growth industry
Was Social disorder
And exporting soldiers

EPICS 3

To foreign places
In the shrinking world;
To kill unknown faces

For it was fate's call.
To control a world
Growing so small.

Or so they said.
To know yourself before the fall;
Was the greatest challenge of all.

You must listen to the voice
Create options; a choice;
The thinking brain In your head.

The unified voice;
One voice
Thought process

To avoid
The system
Designed to regress

S.E. McKENZIE

Those not controlling
The process.
Overpriced schools,

Leaving many as fools.
Imprisoned in their own mental torture
Chamber;

Trust was buried
In wasted Paradise;
The psyche-soul was now as cold as ice.

Personal freedom
Was impossible
Without financial freedom;

In the shrinking world;
Devalued currency;
To be free Never to be free;

Would now cost more.
We all knew the lie.
You could count the days

EPICS 3

Until you died
Of Starvation.
No crueler fate

Too late; nothing on your plate
Some hope for power
So they can change the state

Of hate.

Cold and steely
Fake lover
Who turned away;

Not the right religion;
Not in the right circle;
As death came too soon.

THE END

S.E. McKENZIE

DEATH PANEL

EPICS 3

#32. DEATH PANEL

I

Who burnt those people
A long time ago?
Who processed the young

Before they had a chance to grow?

II

In a time called zero
The weaponized; the mechanized;
Took what they could

From the faint hearted;
Now departed;
Changed the time

But not the clock
On the wall.
Tic Toc;

Sue's heart beats to its own drummer;
Isolated Sue
Before her fall.

S.E. McKENZIE

III
Sue screamed out in pain;
Doctor Joe Inc. called her insane;
He said Sue looked quite odd

And disconnected from it all.
Nowhere to live
Her clothes were way too big

No concern for her presentation
Could not afford representation
Perfect specimen for experimentation.

IV
Members meet in a room
Which is dark and full of gloom.
Energy vampires

Push and shove
The Broken People.
Convenience sells;

Self-serving Death Panels;

EPICS 3

Complaint driven
By the Busy Body of the day;
Craving to be Ghetto Queen;

She speculates
To elevate her own social position
While sucking in others to spin

Within her endless negative loop;

Fear mongering and gossiping
Are her tools;
When she is denied

She makes her victims
Look like fools; and we knew
Truth was the enemy of Bias;

While we tried to avoid
The adversary process;
Which the Death Panel projected

Into their Processing Room.

S.E. McKENZIE

While standing on the street corner
Busy Body speculates
Sometimes cruelly;

Elevates her standing;
As Ghetto Queen; Her only way;
To feel important;

For time will soon make
Busy Body obsolete.
Even though she craves to be elite.

Standing by the needle exchange
Ghetto Queen shouts insults
At Sue walking home

All alone in the Negative Zone;
Where the negativity is draining;
Not much effort goes to sustaining

Positivity dies too quickly.

EPICS 3

V
Sue must play along
Pretend that Joe Inc. is right
Even when he is wrong;

Pretend all night;
Pretend until the morning light
Arrives to bring in a new day

Not yet touched
By the Death Panel
Trying to find a way

To fit Sue's case into the billing code.

VI
Social service;
With no social mobility;
Setting Sue up for lower society;

Dr. Joe Inc. complained about Sue's smell;
Dr. Joe Inc. said Sue looked like hell;
Dr. Joe Inc. would micro-manage

Sue as if she were a beast.

S.E. McKENZIE

Dr. Joe Inc.; the micro-aggressor;
Creating; positioning;
Reinforcing a lower social order;

For profit;
As predator;
On Sue's psyche, Dr. Joe Inc. would feast.

Death Panel;
They meet
Without having to greet

Sue trying to prove a negative;
Risk to sanity; consultation
Can be done over the phone

With someone above
In the social pecking order;
No mentor just micro-aggressor;

No social security lawyer
Found in the telephone book;
Go screaming down the street;

EPICS 3

And the moneyed criminal lawyers
Will give Sue another look;
The police will help them book;

While we knew the crime.

Money driven; complaint driven;
Creating a lower social position;
Less competition;

Without social mobility
How can anyone be free?
Micro aggressor

Picks a fight
Causes a fright
And entry into a lower social order.

Death panels stay on call;
For convenience sake.
Writing off Sue but could be you;

Poverty legislated;
Position dictated;
With no way out.

S.E. McKENZIE

Blocking entry
Blocking integration
For a new generation

Without a title.

Creating artificial structure
A disadvantage for one
Is an advantage for another;

Social predator;
Gave Sue a glass of wine at work
Then complained to the higher up

That Sue was drinking at work;
The Nouveau Gestapo was called
And processed Sue that very day;

Never to be unmarked again;
Precious lover never answering her call;
Steely silence made Sue scream;

EPICS 3

Not the right religion
Not in the right circle
Isolation; never selected

Now positioned to be neglected;

Was not seen as a mistake.
Manufactured cause to discriminate
It was money driven;

It was complaint driven;
No complaint was too small;
The micro-managers; the micro-aggressors

Now had a full time job making Sue crawl.

And no money could be made
In social security law;
So Sue was treated like a criminal instead.

Made the fear worse in Sue's head;
In a world where every door
Was now shut in her face day after day;

Often a victim of Ghetto Queen's hysteria
Whenever seen
In a public area.

S.E. McKENZIE

Year after year;
Personal comment
Manufactured consent.

Though there was no smell of alcohol
The Nouveau Gestapo would answer the call
If Sue was labeled alcoholic;

For the new war was not just economic;

In the red-lined district
Where Government sponsored beer
Was always near; a better chance to succeed in business

If you drink with the right people;
Sell to the right people
Complain to the right people.

And a long time ago the busy body of the day
Ghetto Queen, wanted Sue to go away;
And offered her a drink

Then waved a letter in her face,
Accused her of sending it to her place,
In front of everyone in the room

EPICS 3

Sue was mortified
And wished that she had died.
Wondered why someone she admired would lie.

Busy Body then phoned
The Nouveau Gestapo
With her complaint

While Sue was still in shock feeling faint.

From that day on Sue was never the same;
Busy Body said Sue was caught drinking at work;
While Busy Body looked out of the window

Always ready to complain
Whenever Sue was near;
Filled Sue with Fear;

Phoned her friends
Who were always near
And they all put Sue on their list;

To watch;

They were certain that Sue
Was a descendant from
Witches due to her nose

S.E. McKENZIE

Due to her clothes;
The micro-aggressor
Told the under class

Where to sit
And where to stand
And whenever she stared at Sue

She felt fear, she said;
Did not know
What to do, she said.

Phoned the Nouveau Gestapo
To take Sue away;
The vulture cultures were on their way.

Even though Sue just lived down our street
She was not treated like a neighbor
By the wanna-be elite.

Poor Sue;
What could she do:
Now victim of self-fulfilling prophecy

Very few would let her be.

VII

How can anyone be free
In a multi-tier society;
Secret Currency is paid on entry

To Secret Watcher-Society.

We said Sue had the right to live
And society needed to shift
In order to give Sue a lift.

A Two-way gift; growing to be
The best
She could be.

Doctor Joe Inc. disagreed;
And on these cases
He did feed;

Never considered
How self-fulfilling prophecies
Created the gap; created the need;

Sue went to a Human Rights Channel;
And they took her case
But Dr. Joe Inc.'s word was believed

S.E. McKENZIE

As soon as they saw Sue's face.
The Channel had a robot investigator
Listened to what Dr. Joe Inc.'s lawyers had to say

The team of lawyers
Were paid
Thousands of dollars a day

To make the Human Rights Channel go away;
Took out the rule that disallowed
The Human rights Tribunal to make a phone call.

And they said
Sue's fear
Was just in her head.

Hypocrisy;

VIII
Money was being made
In a war
To prevent World War III

So the King of Bling said;
Out of this world context;
Bias was innocent, they said;

False Pride;
Arrogant killer;
King of Bling

The Divine Thriller;
Able to turn
Blood into wine.

IX

We were drafted to fight a war
To prevent a war.
Across the sea;

It was said
They were fighting
For human rights;

So everyone was dressed to kill;
Conflict of interest;
Multiple roles for financial gain.

X

Sometimes Sue screams out in pain
But then the pain
Goes away when she remembers

S.E. McKENZIE

Her lover from days gone by;

And life goes on
Expensively;
And soon Sue will no longer be.

The way she used to be.

For now Sue has a label hanging
From her big toe;
And nothing more we shall know.

Death Panel;
They count all the food
That Sue won't have to eat.

They don't count
The past contribution
And Sue's own interest compounding;

The heartlessness was astounding.

Death Panel;
They will sell the shoes
Off Sue's feet;

EPICS 3

Death panel;
Domain of the elite
Finding a way to fit their desired outcome

Into the Billing Code.

Profit for the shareholders;
Less expense for the taxpayers
Death Panel;

Needed to fit the billing code
In a civilized way
So everyone waves

As sue passes away.
Death Panel remains
Disengaged;

Silently; humanity was estranged;
Never speaking to her;
Just at her;

Never answering her call;
Always making her feel small;
In a world of plenty

S.E. McKENZIE

They were so many
Moving along
On empty.

Moving mountains
Made from mole hills
Micro-aggression; macro-suggestion;

"Don't say
That one day
The billing code will finance

Paid killers;
Don't say the Truth;
In polite society that is rude;

Don't use words like Death that are so crude."

Ordered the King of Bling;
"Pray for power or anything
But the truth;

For Truth is the enemy of Bias."

Death greets Sue at the door
Gone from life
For evermore.

EPICS 3

Sue no longer will exist;
Sue will never be missed;
Or so the Death Panel will say.

World around the mirror;
The world so small;
And getting meaner;

Day by day
The Death Panel
Will shape the way.

Day by day
They find a way
To keep it clean;

They smile
When they tell you how to live
And tell you when to die.

Billing Code
The new bible
In the world where war makers

Say they crave peace;
There is no plan
In the design to make change.

S.E. McKENZIE

Just dollars;
Weaponized; mechanized;
Bureaucracy;

Using the young for cannon fodder.

Contradicting what you experience;
Sheltered on the other side;
Of the glass ceiling;

Just a feeling
Micro-aggressor
Micro-manager

No right of way for Sue.

So smothering;
For Sue
Could no longer scream;

The outcome
Was not measured
For the secret process was not yet covered

Under the billing code.

THE END

EPICS 3

BIGGIE

#33. BIGGIE
I
Time
A circle
The beginning

And the ending; everlasting;
When seen from the sky
By those not yet sleeping inside infinity;

No longer able to touch
Or be touched
The way mere mortals can be.

Vibrating
Pulsating
Now so free.

What we see
Depends
On transparency.

II
She looks into the mirror
She does it everyday
She looks into the mirror

EPICS 3

Cause she was brought up that way.

She sees the reflection
Of herself
In her projection

Of you.
In a world broken in two
By the sad man

Whose heart yearns to be free

From his reflection;
Free from his projection;
Free from his suggestion;

While time ravaged our youth.

Vibrating
Pulsating
Not yet free

Not yet floating inside Infinity.

III

Inaccurate missile;
Small warhead;
Randomness;

Created our luck by chance;
We ducked Demented Society's savagery;
While Nouveau Gestapo stared;

Did not care;
About our vulnerability
Even though big guns were all around.

No Time to dance
Or linger in our youth
We were faced with a terrible truth.

We were not allowed in the polling booth

For Inequity was all around;
We treaded lightly
On hillbilly ground.

Our lives may be shortened
By Big Guns Projections;
Or worse yet, weapons of war

EPICS 3

May turn us into something grotesque;
One day.
We will fade away anyway;

From all of this.

But today we crave Universal Love
And refused
To be demoralized

By the Nouveau Gestapo's Tune.

In a world where the Regulator
Forced our silence;
He relished in his highness.

We could not protest;
Or suggest
A better way.

For the Regulator had the only say.
And the single explanation
To everything.

There was no dictator in the sky.
Time's boundaries
Were sucked away

S.E. McKENZIE

Inside a black hole
No beginning or end
In a timeless soul

Of Infinity;
What one can see
Depends on Transparency.

We walk down the road
Of time
As age aged us savagely.

Love was under attack.
We seldom tired as we watched Love's back
We wanted the best; needed little rest.

We were the lost Generation
Or so the demented rulers said.
We responded to positive sensation

But we were hated instead.
The Regulator
Was like a vacuum

EPICS 3

And many could not grow
Into tomorrow
For the barriers were too many;

We saw the boundaries
Which shrunk our earth
And diminished what could have been

Self-worth.

A beautiful land of great hope
Free from Gestapo's rope;
The Regulator's command.

Created demand
In the only growth industry left
Social disorder.

Weakened by pain;
Empowered by Universal Love;
We knew what we needed

But there was never enough.
The demented lived in fear
Of everything they did not know

S.E. McKENZIE

Or could not remember;
They said we did not belong
And made it so;

Yes, we were not a member

Of the Old Boy's Club
Some members could not remember;
Some carried the weapons which oppress;

People change when under duress;
So afraid to be dispossessed;
For we were still young.

As Youth; we were pushed away;
By the demented;
Empty heads already rented.

The future was promoted
In a state of hypocrisy
Watchers watched but could not see

In this land of mediocracy.
Ghetto Queen touched up her hair
Until it was golden

EPICS 3

Put on her fancy underwear
And stared through people
As if they weren't there;

She laughed as they spoke
So no one ever did;
Whenever they saw her coming

They hid.

To question the big guns
Was a form
Of Heresy; Just like

Questioning Demented Society's savagery.

The demented watchers were too blind to see
The entrance to the path
Which led to a great life

Was blocked by rusty barb wire
And holy gun-fire; so proud were they
When they fondled their Big Guns.

IV

Regulator had immunity;
Compulsive violator of humanity
In his quest to become a god;

Regulator turned back time
As the world grew smaller
And more bitter.

No constitution
In the land was higher
Than the Regulator's command.

V

The Regulator still ruled; still fooled;
The pigs on the mechanical farm.
The one with the biggest gun

Made everyone else run.
It was a crusade;
Big Guns were on parade.

I too had to run from his Killer Gun;
I ran into a foreign land
I hid my face, thought of a place

EPICS 3

I once called home; still unknown to the living;
Where hearts could pulsate
Free; without feeling hate

Or worrying about the future state of Fate.

Timeless and forever changing
Love might live forever
In a place called infinity Plus One.

We were the brave and had no gun;
We all refused to be slaves
To our fear; even though fear was always near.

And fear of others
Separated sisters and brothers;
We were still young enough

To call strangers our neighbors.

Ghetto Queen of mean
Pushed around people
Who were unseen.

"We don't want you here,
Dear";
She would sneer.

S.E. McKENZIE

We knew she was dehumanized too;
For we could see the lie
In every tear that she could not cry.

The barriers were installed;
Made us hungry
Some ate out of garbage bins;

While the Regulator
Locked food away to rot
As Time's touch was gentler to some;

As the ones so fancy
Called us names;
They still were free

To play games;
While we spent
Some of the day

Finding a place to pee.

EPICS 3

VI

Our Links in the food chain
Were broken
Our pain had awoken

Ghetto Queen
And the King of Bling
Looked away

Gave up on today;
The turning point into tomorrow
Would now fade away.

Even though the Regulator
Tried to make it not so;
Time continued to touch

Everything and everyone.
Some were born
And some died;

Many lied
And others cried;
While the Regulator denied

S.E. McKENZIE

That this was so.

Stability
A connection
A chance to be part of the selection

Was now out of reach
For inter-generational
Economic Warfare

Toxic and unfair;
So chaotic when so few
Dare to care;

Marginalization and alienation
Were greater than ever before.
And the Regulator

Said it wasn't so.

VII
The Watchers watched but could not see;
Had very little to say to us;
But we knew Time was on our side.

EPICS 3

The builder of big
Had a new gig;
Just moments before the fall.

Reincarnated dinosaur
Wanted it all
To satisfy

His appetite;
So many had to die
Without a tear to cry;

Without fear they uttered the lie;
We knew the truth
Despite our youth

For Natural law
Was round; a cycle;
Not a flat line;

Kept turning around;
Sometimes frozen in Time;
As smoke and ash blocked the sun;

S.E. McKENZIE

Then their system crashed;
The old food-chain politics
Was now disrupted for evermore

For the store owner had locked the door.

And Time was on our side
Though the Regulator
Said it was not so.

For the smallest survived climate change before;
When the known world was turned upside down
The advantaged became the disadvantaged.

And the ceiling
Turned into a floor
The greatest roar roared no more.

As the biggest of all toppled;
And could not sustain
The appetite which caused so much fright.

The old dinosaur tried
All day and all night;
And us;

EPICS 3

We avoided Society's Savagery

We had nothing to cling on to
So we were free
To walk into the unknown.

VIII
Ghetto Queen
Framed Mary Anne
Into something she was not

Gave Ghetto Queen
A feeling that she was still hot
While the King of Bling

Promised her everything
That money could buy
No reason to make Mary-Anne cry.

"Accept the hate
That changes Fate and social standing,"
Ghetto Queen said

"Consider yourself fired.
We just stick with who we know
The way our Carrot Stick God

S.E. McKENZIE

Tells us to,"
The Ghetto Queen said.
And the man who owned

Castles to rent and buy;
Sold hate
To the highest bidder

Empty space in his head for rent;
So demented
He did not care

When he made so many cry.
They all said their excitement
Was driven by their carrot stick god's energy

More intoxicating than the wine
That was made with the blood
Of the enemy who died covered in mud.

Shaped their frame of mind;
Made many unkind;
The Watchers could not see

EPICS 3

For they were willfully blind.

IX

And we had Love's back;
So she could hold us
When we were under attack;

Our very selves
Were denied validation
We became the children

Of the Lost Generation;
We grew trapped in alienation;
Always looking for something

To give us

A better sensation;
While Nouveau Gestapo
Was throwing around dope

S.E. McKENZIE

Gestapo's rope in the War Economy;
We stood by Love's back;
Holding on to the hope

Only Love was able to give.

While Ghetto Queen
Listened to
The King of Bling

Who prayed for her Psyche-soul;

So Ghetto Queen could die in peace;
After living life at war;
She believed the King of Bling's promise

That her soul would live for evermore;
Lost within
Her steely four chambered heart;

She yelled at us
Whenever she saw us
Sometimes she complained to a watcher

Who looked but could not see

EPICS 3

Culture of obstruction
And destruction
Was everywhere

And we tried to block it out
For Love's sake
We had her back.

While the barriers all around;
Cut us from any food supply;
We were starving to death;

We knew we were close
To our last breath
As we held on to Love a little too tight;

All through the night;
We saw the light;
Shining onto our path;

And different directions
Led to different ways;
And different lives

S.E. McKENZIE

At a Crossroad;
And I felt like a moving dot
On a scatter plot

Just a target to be shot.

And I took the path
Which led to the unknown
For I had nothing left to lose.

For Diversity was just the Regulator's word
Patronizing, stigmatizing, dividing;
Just double talk behind the sneer

Projecting fear;
Watchers always near;
Always watching but could not see

Their own hypocrisy.

Manufactured a skid row;
The Regulator divided a whole city;
Did not care about our sorrow;

In the prison style city;
Bulldozing what was not pretty;
Creating negative situations

EPICS 3

With unfair accusations.
And we never had a chance
To increase our social standing there.

As they closed down the schools
The ones who stayed grew into fools;
Stuck in the prison city;

The Nouveau Gestapo
Stared at us
With steely eyes

That marginalized;
For the Regulator
His highness; contrasted

With our lowness;
Time around us
Froze into slowness.

The Final Hour
Turned our world upside down
While our progress moved backwards.

S.E. McKENZIE

The Watchers watched
But could not see
As we tried to save our

The Watchers watched us
While some grew demoralized;
Lost their self-esteem;

Could not put together
Their broken dream
For the Regulator

Manufactured Skid Row.
Nowhere left to grow
Without sorrow.

The Watchers watched
Standing under the sign
Which buzzed out the word diversity.

The Watchers watched
Fate go by without a tear in their eyd;
Easier to hate than to innovate;

EPICS 3

The boundary of our growth
Stopped at every barrier
Which was said to beautify

Though we knew the lie

Fences were all around
To keep the nature in
Which was dying and could not thrive;

For Nature too was not allowed to be free.

THE END

S.E. McKENZIE

SPINNING

#34. SPINNING
I

I saw my dreams so out of reach;
Spinning in the sky;
I asked them why;

Then my dreams came tumbling down

And fell to the ground
Without a sound
Without a cry;

The snake
Was toyed with
By a sharp stick;

Outraged
It circled its prey
Though the prey tried to runaway.

The snake looked at me
And then looked at Ted
Who was counting his wealth left by Fred;

S.E. McKENZIE

Fred never met Ted;
The grandson born
Years after Fred was dead.

With a tear in his eye, the snake said,
"I have been so misunderstood
Day by day,"

Ted looked away
Not interested
In a word that snake had to say.

Ted went on counting his wealth;
Product of Fred's sacrifice and virtue;
And the freedom

That was still left;
Before Fred passed away.
Though no one had the time of day

To say goodbye;
Fred did not cry;
While the children played in the rain

They had nowhere else to go;

EPICS 3

While toxic towns
Conditioned people
To stay guarded

While smiling sweetly;
Professional agitators
Held hands with social engineers;

And they all came around;
Stomping their feet on the ground
Commenting on our appearance

Stirring up fear;
Ruining the atmosphere
Whenever they were near.

And Fred once said,
"I will always spin with you,
Where ever I may be;

In the sun;
Where life must have begun;
Making us a derivative

S.E. McKENZIE

Of One.
Don't need
No sum zero games

No more;
In the place I will be
For evermore."

While the ragged people on earth
Stayed in rusty vans below their worth;
Parked on land

Out of sight
Of the Power Clique's
Might;

The rain turned to snow.
As the decay grew
Behind the fence

The Power Clique
Had erected;
The forgotten people shivered;

EPICS 3

Left out in the cold
As they grew old;
The power Clique

Lied as the poor people died;
Victims of the growing decay
Accelerating day by day.

Ted no long lived
In the country of his descent;
That land was left far behind;

So proudly;
A long time ago.
Before the name change.

Now, the new land
Is developed
For rent;

II
And day by day; the ragged people
Behind the fence were forgotten;
While decay

S.E. McKENZIE

Made so much go rotten.

Culture of obstruction
And provocation;
Hot passion was no longer the fashion.

But you must never speak out loud;
For the Power Clique
Do not want to remember you;

As you really are;
The power Clique
Make war;

Not love;
For they are perpetually angry;
They watch but cannot see;

They bait
But cannot communicate
For they are living

In a killing machine;

EPICS 3

Brought up to be mean;
So well dressed;
They laugh at the dispossessed;

So wrongly assessed;
How they love
To torment and oppress.

III

Channeled through heartlessness
We spin;
You touching me; we spin;

Holding on to our skin
We spin
We do not bleed

Or die in need;
We spin
To create

Momentum;
And one day
We will win

The race
While keeping
Pace;

Avoiding the face
We see all over the place.
We walk with grace;

Down the path
We learn to love
You and me;

Each one of us;
We spin;
Through all this trouble;

We spin;
Through all this rubble;
We spin.

IV
After Ted builds his wall;
And leaves us far behind
We vow not to fall

EPICS 3

Nor be baited
By those
Who want us hated;

We will spin
Around one sun
Where life must have begun;

On this earth, we share her worth.

Love will show us how;
Give us enough strength
To spin;

We will build
The momentum;
We will let it begin;

From the disruption caused
As they watched but would not see
The disaster in motion

That they created
While they were insulated
From our pain;

S.E. McKENZIE

The children played out in the rain
They had nowhere else
To go;

And it was beginning to snow.

Traffic like a snake
Goes by so fast, never slow.
We know our world

Cannot last.
Careless as they see;
Careless as they speak;

Careless as they chart
The map
That creates our path.

We spin
Like dots on a scatterplot
Before the aftermath.

We spin to project our momentum;
We crawl under the wall;
No matter how tall;

EPICS 3

First one out
Might spill
Their blood in the mud;

We are the forgotten ones.
Only in peace
Will we be free;

We refuse to be dispossessed
Underdressed
A victim to be oppressed;

Their crime can never be confessed;
Just hidden behind the fence;
As time flew by;

The Power Clique
Was so elated;
Happily living

In their world so petty and gated;

Cost of living was now inflated;
The devaluation had begun;
Under one sun;

S.E. McKENZIE

Drugs were piped into the water supply
Unintentionally;
Made many bloated and sedated;

Between rigid rules
That gave power to fools
A tree became uprooted

Leaving a hole wide open;
Into it a life was stolen
Found dead and frozen;

As the wind changed
Torrents flew by;
As Fred started to cry;

Water soaked into the ground;
But us;
Still had the might to be free

As the Power Clique
Grew their new
Social Order

EPICS 3

They left us out in the cold
As we grew old;
Decay grew behind the fence.

Technology
Replaced
Many;

To fit into the new command
That was taking over the land
Controlling demand

The Power Clique tyrannized
With forced guardianship
Of the living;

Decay was unforgiving;

Growing at a rate
So individualized
Controlled by the Power Clique's force;

So collectivized;
The only way to be civilized;
The Power Clique said;

S.E. McKENZIE

"Only the crazy
Listen to their own voice
Buried in their head.

For there is only
One way;
Our way,"

The Power Clique said

While the decay grew;
And ate
Whoever stood in its path;

We were the victims
Of the aftermath;
Now many

Did not even have access to a bath.

As the Power Clique
Dominated
In their one-way world

That spread;
With the superhighway
Where cameras

EPICS 3

Were everywhere
Taking multiple snaps
At the same time.

There was the right way
And the wrong way;
No room for common sense to linger;

The Power Clique knew how
To smile sweetly
As they killed;

But could no longer innovate;
Decay was in the air
And everywhere;

Grew day by day;

The Power Clique were so out of touch,
For their power was able to insulate
Them; so sheltered from the reality of others;

How they laughed
As they grew richer
And the poor grew poorer;

S.E. McKENZIE

The Power Clique had Monopoly Power
To cause prices
To inflate

For their friends;
Were always ready
To make amends;

It was true;
Our future was in decline;
The thought of it

Could burn out your mind;
Negativity was the Power Clique's tool;
Toxic Energy;

To not question it
Made you a fool;
While the Power Clique watched

They could not see the process so cruel;

For they had grown to be
Too
Willfully blind.

EPICS 3

Behind the wall;
No longer seen
As neighbors;

Sisters and brothers
Living inside a living universe
Which some said cared;

And shared its bounty;
Adding value
Day by day;

While the Power Clique
Told us to go away
And not be seen;

The world that we knew
Was getting mean
Some tried to destroy our self-esteem

Tried to drive us to suicide.

During the careless days
Where they watched in a daze;
But could not see.

S.E. McKENZIE

Made them so proud out loud;
For they controlled fate
Could create the power to insulate.

The children cried all night;
Left alone in a place Fred had built
Many years ago;

Some just had
Enough money
To pay the rent;

So
They no longer
Had to live in a tent;

The snake
Was never welcome
In any neighborhood;

Every door has been closed
By the Power Clique;
How can the meek

EPICS 3

Inherit anything?"
The snake said
Years after Fred was dead;

To succeed
You must be
Opportunistic

Holding on
While the world is spinning all around;
Holding on to your ground

While you are still winning.
I am full of life
And I have seen

Many fooled by their sadness;

Too many victims
With broken dreams
That were never lived;

For life is a circle;
Spinning around;
Left in a cruel world

S.E. McKENZIE

Where you never belong;
Stuck behind the fence
There is little opportunity

While Ghetto Queen
Loves to tease
With her wealth;

Loves to break promises
Creating anger;
Her tool so cruel;

Designed to burn out the mind.
Some would be
Caught in the trap

And would lose their sense
Of harmony
Stunted for evermore;

Not able to grow to be
What could have been
Before;

EPICS 3

V
The best you could be;
Your full potential;
To gain a credential;

Decay grew faster;
As the Power Clique laughed
At what they had done;

Their gated world
Now had more sun
While ours was covered in shadow

And sorrow;

So stagnant; could not grow nor progress
While today was turning into tomorrow;
The world was spinning too fast;

Its ground
Stomped upon
By the mechanical pig;

Leaving bones
All alone
In a hole

S.E. McKENZIE

Dug with a heart of stone.

The warhead
Was flying and crying
In the sky;

A tool for a fool;
The mean
Have monopolistic rule

Hiding their roots
Buried so deep
In the ground;

Hoping Truth had lied.

Lost in forgotten memories
That thrived
Decades ago.

Silently died
Without a sound; after Fred's
Heart could no longer pound.

You must not speak

EPICS 3

Of the unseen;
Steely Beast;
So cruel

Under the sea
Living
In a rusty submarine.

VI

Cult of fear
Designed by
The nouveau

Social Engineer
Was always near
We spin to avoid what we fear;

We are a moving dot
On a scatter plot;
As we spin

Momentum
Creates
All we've got;

S.E. McKENZIE

We spin
To avoid
What we fear;

We spin
As we take flight;
We spin

To avoid a fight

With Ghetto Queen
Creeping around
Controlling her ground

Destroying any chance
To relate;
How she loves to bait;

Looking for prey;
We are out of sight
We spin

As one into the night;
Waiting for the morning light;
To hold us in Nature's warmth.

EPICS 3

VII
The monolithic
Mechanical Pig;
Watches but cannot see;

Hears but cannot listen;
Fear loops around his mind;
Sadistic; simplistic; unkind;

Nothing of value to sell
Except the knowledge
To engineer fear;

No space for Common Sense to linger
While Ghetto Queen
Has you wrapped around her finger;

So able to manufacture consent;
So unable to invent;
How she loves to torment;

"If you don't do exactly as I say;
I will psychologically
Damage

S.E. McKENZIE

She says with a sneer.
We no long live
In the country of our descent;

I will decide the cost of your rent;
I am the one
In charge of consent;"

Ghetto Queen
Looks so cool
With her hannah red hair;

If you don't fear her
You will soon be turned into
A tool for a fool;

She throws out insults
To control our space;
The place where we hide

Our face.
Still, we walk in grace
Under one sun.

EPICS 3

Ghetto Queen
Is so overdressed;
She is so elite

And she loves to oppress;
We know we should not speak;
Act as if we are not there;

For she can only share her hate;
Loves to bait;
Doesn't try to communicate;

And she holds
The power of the flame
How she loves to inflame

Our fear;
To lose ourselves;
In the fear she loves to spread;

She looks at us
We know
She wants us dead.

VIII

She whispers at you
As you leave the bank
So proud to remind you

Of your rank;
Ghetto Queen owns it all;
No room for market correction;

Only the Ghetto Queen
Has to the power
Of selection;

How she loves to control
With her Negative
Suggestion;

We hear the Ghostly voice say
"For thirty years
I had to pay triple net

EPICS 3

And what did I get;
When I was too old to work
They took all I had

Then just let me die;"

Public space; no longer free;
Loss of Privacy;
We fight for our sanity;

Us; Ragged People;
Too weary to take
Another step

Ghetto Queen;
So mean; would destroy
All your tomorrows;

While crushing your dream.

Baiter; hater;
Instigator;
Inflator;

Of the cost of living

In a rat hole gets steeper;
She gets her way;
Every day;

Enjoying her pay day
Making Ragged People's life
Hell;

Making it harder to buy
Instead of increasing
The market supply.

IX

Spinning around
With feet firmly on the ground;
Not allowed to speak

Cannot make a sound
We are too weak;
We spin

To create momentum
To surround us
While the test

EPICS 3

Is in motion;

Cannot rest;
When the day comes
A new name is given to you;

If you complain;
Ghetto Queen will show distain
Cause you pain

For the billing code
Is the new bible that must be followed
Without a grumble

Lie down now
While you worry about your sanity
While others say

You have been lost in depravity;
Keep your eyes on the road
See the new car

Paid by the billing code
See the advertisement
On the license plate;

S.E. McKENZIE

Run out of the door
Before
It is too late.

The meeting
Does not include you
So they will never know

The facts
That made
Who you are, true.

X

Looking for something to live for
In a world
Dominated by war;

News that made you
Feel so bad;
Helps you forget

How much you can't have
Which could have changed your life;
So the world could grow to be

EPICS 3

Less sad.

Seen too much
From the baiter who loves to hate;
Seen too much behind the barrier

Which limits our fate;
Slows down momentum;
As our energy is captured

And frozen in time.

Even more energy is captures
Through the Public Internet Carrier
Following our every move;

Captures images of our faces too;
On cameras
Snapping shots

All at the same time.

XI
Mean Girls
Here and there
Putting on make-up;

S.E. McKENZIE

Doing their hair;
Sexualize who they want
As if the other person

Is not there;
Drives some to suicide
As they take over space

After they brush on
A different face;
A new look;

For Facebook.

XII

Nouveau Gestapo's sneer;
The first step
In a campaign of smear;

Demoralized for pay
And a stay
In a private resort;

EPICS 3

On Christmas Day
Mean Girl
And the watchers stand all around;

Looking at homeless people who are down;
"You look like a recovering alci,
Here is a bottle of wine;"

How Ghetto Queen laughs
As she walks by the ragged people;
Wearing their Goodwill clothes;

Just garbage to some;
She whispers;
An insult in someone's ear;

The ragged person
Responds in fear
As Ghetto Queen laughs

Ragged Person is now sucked into her game;

Now the ragged person will be
The one to blame;
The Ghetto Queen

S.E. McKENZIE

So well fed;
She smiles so sweetly;
After she adds insult to injury;

The feeling of fear is now so near;

Ghetto Queen's life goes on the same;
Loving the power to insult after injury;
Gives her a feeling of joy;

For other people's
Emotions
Are just her toy;

Only Ghetto Queen can win;
Nouveau Gestapo drives by
And says "hi,

Why don't you make them cry;
Make them wanna die,
If they disappear

Our beautification project
Will be closer to complete
And then we will enjoy

EPICS 3

What it means to be elite."
Ghetto Queen nods;
As she holds on

To her Poinsettia tightly;
Just slightly toxic;
If a pet does ingest

Consultation fees
May apply;
Ghetto Queen

Holds life and death
In her hands;
She feels so mighty;

Manipulator of emotions so deep
Better to let
Sleep.

XIII

Threatening an assault
Is never a tort
For the Mechanical Pig;

S.E. McKENZIE

As the Ghetto Queen
Spins her hype
Shaping a biased stereotype;

Once a year.
The revolving door
Lets a few out.

Now broken and torn and worn;
The list for everything
Channels the dispossessed

Through identifiable labels
Often misused
And abused;

Labels to disconnect
From those
Whose status depends

On being over-dressed;

EPICS 3

Money; quantified power to control one's fate;
If only for a moment;
Before cost of living

Spirals out of control
After oil markets crash;
We all wait for the next boom;

The flags are waving;
We are told
We are heading for doom;

That we are misbehaving by living.

In a program of beautification
The ghetto queen loves making a scene
To show her superior position

To us;
It was Tyranny
That we tried to resist;

She drove right into us
But missed;
We said something to a passerby

S.E. McKENZIE

But she put her nose up in the air;
Acted as if we weren't there;
Confirmed how the Power Clique is everywhere;

Process of bad decision making
By others who do not care;
Leads to despair;

And to disparity so unfair;

Fabricating negative suggestion;
No time to question;
Too much rush

In all this congestion.
The war generation
Played it like a game;

So collectivized
And dehumanized
No curiosity

Left.

EPICS 3

No positive imagination spent;
We lived in a world
Of manufactured consent;

No relationships forming;
Just Control Gangs swarming.
Some said it was the end of the world

And were making it so;

And love had so far to go;
For all was now controlled
No room

For common sense to grow;
As today flowed into tomorrow;
We could not sleep;

We were too cold;
Growing old;
Many were shifting

Into an impersonal role;

S.E. McKENZIE

As the Power Clique's domain
Was just a place of pain;
Where decay

Turned everything into rot;
While Ghetto Queen
Looked into the mirror,

And then painted her face again.

THE END

EPICS 3

REBEAT

#35. REBEAT
I

ReBeat; goes my heart;
Repeat; we tear each other apart;
Defeat; only one can win

At Sum Zero game play.

Tic Toc
Goes my clock;
Time does not knock

But only barges in to create a shock;
Impure Fusion needs Fission;
Still a hard decision

For there is an ocean
Inside me; attracts; reacts;
Pulls me back and forth with my inner tides;

Splitting; competing
Towards Sum Zero.
No one needs to be a hero;

EPICS 3

Dodging time's touch;
Just another
Sum Zero game to play;

Blame the loser for losing;
Praise the winner for winning.
Logical; philosophical;

Sum Zero game play;
So practical
For those living in the Ivory Tower

Over there;
Why should they care
About here?

While we all had
Our eyes closed
In prayer; surrounded by Fear.

Pete buried what was left of his past;
Could no longer climb
The steep steps fast;

S.E. McKENZIE

Leading to the top of the Ivory Tower;
"Do you really have to ask
If Hate is older than Love?"

I heard him scream;
Awoken from his broken dream.
"Do you really care?

You, so protected up there."

Then I knew, what old man Pete
Must have been going through;
Now, I could feel his tear drops

Accumulating around my feet.
Old man Pete;
Always acting as if he were elite;

Today, he faced defeat.

Hate so toxic filled the air;
Strategically placed
In every war and everywhere.

Sending us back to zero
With nowhere else
To go.

EPICS 3

Few would dare to care.
While Hate was consuming Goodwill
Just to irritate Fate;

Made Love come too late;
As Hate initiated even more Hate;
So much more than ever before.

Destroying Harmony
While Fear and Despair
Crushed Talent before it could grow;

From today into tomorrow
All that was left was sorrow;
If it had not been for the Hope

We had to borrow.

Many were hanging
By Gestapo's rope
Fooled by Gestapo's dope.

S.E. McKENZIE

II
Everyone is waiting for a miracle;
But all I see
Is how they crushed

The Tree
Of Unity.
Now, how will we ever be free?

Stakeholder;
Life blood
Of every entity;

Spilled all over the ground;
The shock
Made my heart pound;

Too many Souls to count;
Hanging
From the Tree of Unity;

By Gestapo's rope;

EPICS 3

They were fooled
By Gestapo's dope
And are now no more;

No longer able to touch
All the things
That they used to love so much;

Ghosts flying into the atmosphere;
Up above and not so clear
Sort of free from all this fear.

And Gestapo
Never had to shed a tear
The bodies were not even near;

He was the ruler; that never had to lead;

He was the fooler inspired by greed;
Ignoring all the underfed that he refused to feed;
That were overkilled

In all this greed.

S.E. McKENZIE

Sum Zero game was his only strategy;
Never meant to prevent a tragedy;
Just a mindless travesty;

Escalating as World War Three;

War Machinery
Without a heart;
ReBeat cannot start;

Repeat; History
One more time
Again.

As Pete refused defeat;
He climbed the steps
Hidden inside

The Ivory Tower;
Soon he could see
So much more;

If only they would have opened the door.

EPICS 3

Toxic Town so divided and torn apart;
Everyone wants control
So they micro-manage their Soul;

Freezing motion in time;
Confusion
While impure Fusion needs Fission to start.

Avoid relating
To the unknown
Unkempt generation;

So Frozen in time
All they could do was shiver and linger;
Trapped inside their two faced world

They could not guard their back
As they played
The Sum Zero game.

Defeat; no one can win;
As they all forgot to feed the beast
That now must hunt;

S.E. McKENZIE

Too complicated
For Bureaucracy
To stop.

Old man Pete;
Black hair dye; not much to eat;
Grumbles as he stumbles in the Ivory Tower.

Old man Pete
Cannot defy
The Force of Time.

Never walking lightly;
Absentee landlords
Roll in their dough

From Micro Plots
Packed and stacked
From the ceiling to the floor;

All on top of each other;
Not much room for more;
Nowhere else to go.

EPICS 3

The ones so moneyed;
Had only one motivator
And it was their greed;

Leaving nothing for their brother.
In the wasted land;
So many left behind;

Looking for a way to feed
All of those
Breaking down in need.

Even though spring
Was in the air
Cruelty was called fair;

For it was everywhere.

As the flood gates opened their doors;
The Gong Show began.
In Backward Nation

Can only predict the past;
Always afraid
Of being last;

S.E. McKENZIE

The King of Bling
Stands at his
Bully Pulpit

While impure Fusion
Needs Fission
To start.

Perfect Platform
To project
His Holy Agenda;

To us; Just another secret;
Everyone wants
Power; so they take it from others;

To win
The Sum Zero
Game.

So willing to let another
Lose the most
In order to win the most;

EPICS 3

"I will blame a Holy Ghost.
When this Sum Zero game
Hurts you the most,"

Said the crying child;
Lost in a loop
Of destroyed morale;

Has no one else to cling to
But
The King of Bling.

Polarized;
Stigmatized;
Too easy to lose;

For people on same side;
Sum Zero Game;
Is close to suicide;

Too easy to play.

S.E. McKENZIE

If it were not for God watching;
And the hope for a ride to Heaven
And everlasting Life;

Where the dead poets live after life;
Many dying by their own hands;
Grew weaker than their words

Which imprisoned their minds;

Hate; toxic mind control;
Between the haves and have nots;
And those that spin the loop;

Some get lost inside their minds;
Others get lost in the Wasted Land;
While Nouveau Gestapo

Stomps out the Beat.
So many
Are too willing to repeat.

While spinning the loop.
To stay positive
In the Wasted Land

EPICS 3

That stopped believing in love
A long time ago;
When life's beat was slow

But hard;
Rhythmic interaction
In the Wasted Land;

Many followed the God of Love;
Not yet captured
By the God of War;

So able to rule;
But could not lead;
For there would have been too many

For him to feed.

While the Wasted Land fell;
Burned
Like Hell.

Two sides
To everything
Or so it seems

S.E. McKENZIE

As water flows out
Into streams
That will never be free

For the water is trapped in currents
Controlled by the pull
Of the sun and moon.

Hear the screams;
Everything is now gone
That they worked for;

The control freaks laugh out loud
For they have won
The game of Sum Zero;

The circle must now be respun
For it can never be undone
Without losing a life.

A life worth fighting for;
Now we too
Believe in War.

EPICS 3

Just the way so many have done before;
For we want the beat
To go on for evermore;

To never stop;
For life as we know it
Will then stop too.

III

Wasted Land under a new command;
Depopulation
Began when they brought in strangers

From a distant land
Who began to kill
All those who could no longer

Pay their bill;

The locals screamed out in pain
As they realized
That they were betrayed

S.E. McKENZIE

One more time again,

For public property was never free;
Now privately
Micro-managed

By the power clique;
Blurring civil with criminal;
Blurring an assumption with a lie;

Blurring suicide
With fatal error;
Class distinction

No more.

Without a face
Or a place
To call one's own;

Even the dead had nowhere to go;
They roamed
Unable to touch

Everything that they had loved so much.

EPICS 3

IV
Noble Man;
Just a man of fiction;
No longer shocked were we

To find the real man not noble at all;
Gaining his advantage
Through exploiting fear of others;

Even his sisters and brothers;

So much fear was flowing
And showing
Surrounding the Lost

Who were hiding in the Wasted Land;
Descendants of the enemy
Who changed sides;

A long time ago.

His Negative Bias was beginning to show;
Burnt the only bridge found
Now we have to walk around

S.E. McKENZIE

The current
Which is violent at times;
Could pull us all in.

V

Fusion
The power of the sun and stars;
Reaction to two hydrogen atoms

Combined
Could blow my mind;
Distance

Is what keeps me safe;
Only for a moment;
Until my life is crushed

By the Sum Zero game;
Then I must
Start all over again.

VI

Fission
Escaping neutrons
Strike

EPICS 3

Terror in all they surround;
Melting the ground;
Consuming itself.

Fission to set off impure Fusion;
Process to fit into a missile;
But all I see is a tool for a fool

Lost in delusion;

Who can only rule;
But never lead;
Turning away;

With nothing good to say;
Closing his eyes
As his people starve.

THE END

S.E. McKENZIE

REBOUND

#36. REBOUND: IF YOU CAN

I

The sunrise stayed for the day;
Then set in the usual way;
The door was open

Like it never had been before;

Water was dripping and it was all over the floor;
I did not know from where
And I couldn't find anyone who would care.

The fog crept in
And I lost my way
No one listened to a word I had to say.

So alone;
My heart felt like stone;
The tide was coming in

And no one would let me win;
That was the day after
The Starman died;

S.E. McKENZIE

The day a noble and a gentle man was pulled
Back into his new home
In the sky.

For it was his turn to fly
To a place
One could never reach alive.

All he left me was the starlight
That I could only see
During the night

When I could not sleep
And could not dream
When the silence made me want to scream.

II

Such a brave Contradiction
Against the Pull
Which drives us

To flow against the tides;
Inside out
No one left to shout out for me

EPICS 3

For the Starman
Could now
Defy gravity

In dignity;

The same Force
Which kept me
Grounded on this Earth.

But left me all alone
Now it was up to me
To grow wings of my own.

And the Lady with the Rose
Saw the light too
That the Starman had left behind

To shine light onto my paths
And to warm my heart
So I would not drown

In the ocean deep inside
Pulling me
From tide to tide.

S.E. McKENZIE

The light that Starman left behind
Strengthened
My heart

Still pulsating
When torn apart;
That was the power

Of his light upon my heart.

III
The Starman would now discover
Our Universal Source.
There might be one;

There might be another;

Few would ever know;
A Source more than a Super Ego
Clashing into the night;

Picking a fight
With those who could never win
Without the Lady with the Rose;

We waited until she arose

EPICS 3

In the aftermath;
When manufacturing despair
Was meant to take over the loser's mind;

We found
A way
To rebound;

Now stuck
On this dead end street
In this dead end town;

Manufactured to be that way;

When we lost our right of way;
We could not progress; while those
On the other side of the tracks

Just turned away;
Never having anything good to say; to us;
They could not see the Lady with the Rose

Who arose
From the aftermath
That was left behind.

S.E. McKENZIE

They could watch but could not see
The dead end road to Snobocracy;
Some were below and some were above

In this dead end town
There was too much hate
And not enough love.

So I looked up above
And saw the starlight
That the Starman had left behind;

With us;
For now he was living somewhere above
This tortured land

Under the command
Of money and gold
Tattered and torn

While allegiance was sworn
To the Carrot-stick God
That we could never see;

Some had sworn a life of secrecy;
For Money had written
In God We Trust

All over it;
The bill was our life line
So we knew that we must

Have blind trust
If we were to rebound
From Zero.

IV

It was early in the morning;
So we were able to
Avoid the swarming.

I saw so much food
I could not believe my eyes;
Half of it had been discounted too;

I was going to buy some just for you.
Then I heard someone say
That the food must be thrown away

For food costs more than people can pay.
Devaluation; a hurt sensation;
Was the only way; in a land crippled in hate and debt;

S.E. McKENZIE

Economy zombified;
Another Grumpy old Man
Had just lied;

Another starving child had just died;
"The worst was yet to come,"
I heard the Grumpy Old Man say

As he pushed a blue trolley carrying all the food away;
Then I saw many more Grumpy Old Men;
Here and there and everywhere;

Too bitter to have a gentle touch;
For their anger
Protected them from the fear

That was so near
And bombarded space
Here and there and everywhere.

They took all the food away and there was so much;
I asked why;
And the Grumpy Old Man said, 'That is the rule;

EPICS 3

To not obey makes you a fool; the food has expired
And will be thrown away."
The Grumpy Old Man's hate made him so tired

Soon he too would be expired.

V

In this land of snow
The Mechanized Warlords
Told the rest of us where to go;

Thrown over the fence;
Without a defence;
Nothing made sense.

As the Dead Cat
Bounced back; it rebounded from Zero;
Defying the negative trend;

Momentarily;
Thought it had found
A long lost friend

S.E. McKENZIE

In a Sleeping Bear.
Just another loop
Leading to a dead end.

Just another wall
To confine youth;
As the dictator

Tried to break her mind;
The Lady with the Rose
Who had arose

Understood the value of self-worth;
While Nouveau Gestapo screamed into the night
The Starman was above sharing his light

During another act of war below;
Crushing self esteem
Destroying the dream;

Adaption to insane society
Made many turn away
For there was no inn

EPICS 3

Or home
To begin
The journey from.

While the Starman shone his light
Onto our path
The Lady with the Rose

Cried tears from above
When she saw the sorrow creep into tomorrow;
The aftermath of another act of war.

VI

Some said they could believe
In what they could not;
Some said hypocrisy

Was better than doubt;
Others said the truth
Would never be let out;

For what we had never seen,
We could not perceive;
Some lied anyway

To belong to the gang
Who jumped over the fence
Every Sunday night;

To start a fight
With those who could never win
But were left behind;

Bruised and accused;
Caught in the loop
That had no end.

As the Dead Cat
Bounced off the wall to rebound from Zero;
It thought it had found a friend

In the raging bull.

VII

If only the Starman could
Come down to join us
One more time

We would dance our youth away;
For we know our youth will not stay
And one day it will fade away;

EPICS 3

And make room for the new;
If only the Starman
Could tell us what he knew;

Then we would know
If there was anything at all
Behind the wall

Between life and death;
The circle which spins Infinity;
A space where we have no breath

Left to share;
Beyond
The grave,

If he could tell us
About the things beyond matter
We might feel more brave

And grow to be less sadder;

We would listen now; too;
So curious about what he knew
And where he had been;

S.E. McKENZIE

While our hearts pound
He may hear our sound
Then we will know part of him

Is still around;
Near our ground;
For the life cycle seems to be

Always round.

If he could tell us
What he has seen;
We would then know

If Heaven was just a dream;

What we know
And what we sew
Will surely grow

From Today into Tomorrow;
While the tears falling from the sky
Reminded us that the Lady with the Rose

Would never impose.
Even though she could see all the acts of war;
More Brutal than ever before;

EPICS 3

Left many without a home
With a heart now as cold as stone;
And how could we care

For the Universal Force
Which kept our heart pounding
So mysteriously;

So mightily
Could Unify
Those trapped in the Domain ruled by the Lie.

Still the Universal Force could bind;
Make us more kind;
Less blind than the grumpy old master-mind.

If Starman didn't mind.

If I could only know
What Starman was doing now
I would see

What it was really like to be free,
To be
You and me.

VIII

I had to be true to me;
I could not lie
About what I could not see

Just to belong;
It was wrong
Did not make me strong

Though I would have let
Starman borrow
A tomorrow

From me
If it could have been done;
It would have been like

Having the power to share the sun;

Though the control freaks
Would never understand
Things they could not command

For life was above supply and demand.
Thought they were connected
To the power up above

EPICS 3

They forgot about love
So they did not care
How they shaped fate everywhere.

While the Lie would string us along;

And I could never feel
Or touch the space inside infinity;
So electrifying while still alive;

Possibly terrifying to those left behind on Earth;
Still trapped in hypocrisy;
They watched but could not see;

They said they knew
People they would never talk to;
Growing hypocrisy on the dead end street;

Slum power to dehumanize;
Gave the grumpy old man energy;
As he lived another day while dodging decay.

There was no other way;
He was rotting day by day;
Hidden in his Snobocracy;

S.E. McKENZIE

The dead end mind knew no other way;
Now willfully blind;
Doing things that were more than just unkind.

The tyranny
Of negativity
Would shut out the power

To renew
Me and you
That Unknown Force for ever free

The power Starman tried to share
Once he knew
He was ready to climb into Infinity too;

Electrifying sometimes terrifying;
The Force we could only know;
After we pass; we would be free

From this world where few
Could really care
For they did not dare.

IX

The air was polluted
And so was the heart
Behind the wall;

Looking down
So tall;
Making us

Feel so small.
As Starman
Was looking down

Smiling radiantly
We could not see
For the light

Would blind our eyes.
Pure light so bright;
For it was Starlight;

In the dead of night
It lit up everything in sight;
Until the sunrise brought in the new day

S.E. McKENZIE

In the usual way;
The sun would stay
All day

And then the sun would set
And fade away.
Now we knew

What Starman was trying to say
While we all looked away;
For he was now home.

He had joined the source
Of all resource;
A new recourse.

For us too.

X

Politics of Dehumanization
Grab the ball; don't you fall;
The Sum Zero game must be played

To win;
If you lose
Pick up the pieces and go back

EPICS 3

To where it all began;
Though the cards are stacked
Against you;

In the fools game
Take the 1% chance
To leap ahead;

You must jump over the fence
To see what is over there
In the other world

Where Gestapo told us all
That we would fall
If we tried to belong;

But he was wrong;

For we are now one;
In one world
Still young;

Still growing
Into something new
From the energy Starman left behind.

S.E. McKENZIE

Gave us strength so we would not drown
In the ocean inside
Pulling us from tide to tide.

For life
Was too short
To give up so soon;

For the sunshine
Would be here
By noon

And the God of War
Found
That the best feeling in the world

Was Love;
So he made a trade;
And all weapons were transformed

Into plowshares;
And there was Hunger
No more.

THE END

EPICS 3

FRAMED

#37. FRAMED
I

Framed; Blamed; Named
Then came the diagnosis
At two hundred dollars an hour

"One day Woody may go psychotic."
Doctor Joe Inc. said
As Mary Joe gasped;

There is something wrong

With Woody's head;
There is somewhere
He would rather be instead.

So don't talk to him any more
When you see him;
Run out of the door;

Mary Joe's face will turned into a sneer
Cause her heart
Felt so much fear;

EPICS 3

After the diagnosis
Was put on the internet for all to see
Who would you rather be?

Someone who still had liberty
And a chance for True love
And a happy family

Someone who had a chance
For riches and glory
And a happy ending

To their story?

II

Woody wanted to be
In a place
Where only the sky was blue

A place where few hold a grudge
And even fewer
Judge.

For only peace of mind
Helps Woody feel free to be
More loving and kind;

S.E. McKENZIE

While the watchers stay willfully blind;
We don't watch
What we shouldn't see

And we think that is the way
It always should be.
But Woody was now all alone;

His True Love wouldn't answer the phone;

So afraid of Woody's new diagnosis
At two hundred dollars an hour
Buried alive in a negative file;

At the bottom
Of Doctor Joe Inc.'s pile;
He left it there without a smile.

III
Now the diagnostic tool number five
Would dissect Woody alive;
Just another billing code

To frame a case;
Push Woody onto the road;
Make Woody feel like a toad.

EPICS 3

A diagnosis was so easily made;
In less than an hour;
Without seeing Woody's face;

Woody felt so bad;
He felt so much despair;
He forgot to comb his hair;

He didn't want to be displaced
Or to be disgraced;
Then he sand out loud

Even though it wasn't allowed.

IV

Woody was unwanted as a child
Grew up a little bit wild
He was often sad

Had no clothes to fit;
Was always afraid
Of getting hit.

It had always been that way
Never expecting love to stay.
He felt like a stray;

S.E. McKENZIE

Then one day
He found a guitar
That had been thrown away;

Looked like the guitar;
Had been in a war;
Woody had never seen a guitar

So beat up before.

Woody looked around to see
If there was a trap set up
Nearby

Then his soul took over
And he started to rap;
Then put old guitar on his lap;

And drifted off
Into a nap;
Then he started to sing;

About what he wished he had;
And how much True love
When found would add magic to his sound.

EPICS 3

Woody's voice was so sweet;
He soon was given enough food to eat
And a room to call his own;

He thought;
But it came to not;
His dream would be shot.

He signed the lease anyway;
He signed it in the usual way;
He felt so pleased;

Thought his true love might come back
Even though all he had was a shack
And was still living

On the wrong side of the track;

Then the rich man gave him his book of rules;
And chain-sawed through his ceiling
Turning his world upside down

The ceiling was now the floor
And Woody soon learned the score
How the rich get richer

S.E. McKENZIE

And the poor accept their fate.
While the rich play dumb
While throwing a crumb

On the floor;
Bang the door
Before leaving like before.

No one was kind; they didn't have time;
Cause time was money
And nothing more;

And woody cried behind his door;
He cried harder than ever did before
While he started to thump the floor;

And then was left shaking
All alone behind his door;
Just like the way it was many times before.

He lied in his bed
His eyes were red
Cause he cried a lot;

At times he wished that he would get shot;

As the chainsaw went through his wall
He had no voice;
So he felt so small;

EPICS 3

Then a Nouveau Gestapo accused Woody of using dope;
But Woody knew like we all do;
Dope is the Old Gestapo's rope;

Super fake;
Taking it
Is a huge mistake;

Woody was outraged;
Beyond his age;
He wanted a place to call his own

And he was so sad cause he was all alone;
In a hole
With a hole in the ceiling
And the wall;

He wished on a rap
Then he took a nap
Only escape from all the crap;

Woody just wanted a safe place for his head
To rest
It didn't have to be the best

Place in the world

S.E. McKENZIE

Then Woody sang a song
And a producer came along
With visions of a money tree

He said "Woody let us make a deal
But you must play by my rules;
Your songs have such a great feel;

Could grow a money tree;
Spreading Hope across the land
Into Society and Infinity;

Growing a chance to escape
That hole in the wall
Otherwise could be your fate;

And your voice has so much power
It should be heard
You won't have to live like a sheep

In the herd'
Look at what was done;
Your life was turned upside down

Your power; it was next to none;

EPICS 3

You are so young
You should have fun
But you have nowhere you can run

To; you are all alone; you just have you;
But Woody you have a heart of gold

You will write songs
That will never grow old;
Maybe have a chance to really live;

Or accept your fate;
Such a sad state;
Left all alone;

As your heart turns to stone;
Stuck in that hole in the wall
Owned by a millionaire

Who will never care."

And then he said'
"Don't be too ready to die
In the war that is raging

Oil is over supplied
And Peace and Love
Are things money can't buy

S.E. McKENZIE

So why would they
Give them a try?
Coffee could cost more than oil

If something isn't done
To decrease supply;
Could make many cry."

Woody went to work
All day and toiled
Came back home to see

A pipe
Above sunlight
Bursting from the sky

Into his ceiling;
He did not know
What to call the feeling;

That took over his mind and heart;
So he sang a song;
And his new found guitar played along;

Energy crisis
While the heartless machines
Dug holes so deep

For those machines never had to sleep.

EPICS 3

Legislated poverty;
Trapped some all alone
So no one can see

But Woody knew

What it was like
To have to take
In so much crap.

Just another Millionaire
Who couldn't care
Turned Woody's world

Upside down

Now the glass ceiling
Has become the floor
While Doctor Joe Inc.

Tried to push Woody
Through
The revolving door

THE END

S.E. McKENZIE

LIGHT

EPICS 3

#38. LIGHT
I

Light so bright
Could shine
In the darkest night

On Earth
So much fright
Decay shows its might

While God seems to be out of sight

So it is up to us to transform;
Go beyond the norm
Find shelter in the storm,

To survive
Trouble will grow bigger if we fight
Nature's light must win

Nature; the power to begin
Electricity
Super charged

II

Oh ancient power
More than just
Mysterious gas;

Sun in the sky
Without you
We would all die;

No one left
To cry
Or ask why.

Without you
Matter would have no life
And life would have no matter;

Without light
What would be sadder?
Without the glory; what could we believe in?

Where would we begin?

EPICS 3

The light; we could never touch
So mighty and hot
Blinding to the eyes

When we stare;
So much to share;
If we dare.

Shine through
Humanity's disguise.
Sometimes without hurting the eyes.

Light does not struggle for power
For it is power
And only it can grant true power

To see in front of your feet;
Others will try to delete you;
With light's power they can't defeat you.

Light; we never get enough
Life; tries not to die
In this world of hate and decay;

S.E. McKENZIE

Life would have it no other way;
If life could stay
And never decay

Would sad man
Rage
As age withers him slowly?

What if Nature had made him less lowly?

Grumpy old man
Hurts those below
Those he wants to know; hurts them if he can.

Tells them to stay polite
All night;
Forbids them to say a word;

So they stay out sight; It is his Watcher Job
To not see; individuals
Just the mob.

EPICS 3

Know peace is collective;
Love can only be suggestive;
Crying alone in the night.

Light speeds through time
Curves and bends
In the circle of life;

And without the sun;
We would all die;
No one left to cry

Or ask why.

Feel it and you will never get enough;
Just like love
Softens with a gentle touch

Can hurt so much
When thrown about
Like the Lady with a rose

S.E. McKENZIE

She arose;
While the living were sleeping;
She looked over them while weeping

Holding a rose.
The light was creeping
Back into the sky;

And without the sun;
We would all die;
No one left

. To ask why.

III

Reflect
In the world of neglect
So easy to forget

How we slow down
Decay
Day by day.

EPICS 3

Sad man, angry man
Looks in the mirror
Every day

Hates growing grey
Hates fading away
So jealous of youth's beauty

He forgot his duty;
Though the sun was always there;
Didn't have to care to share its might;

Its light.

Life is round
And will always turn
So don't burn;

Out; Cycles circle
Into seasons of light;

Raging from the sky;
While Nouveau Gestapo won't hear
The other side cry;

S.E. McKENZIE

So caught up
In their mind numbing
Fear;

So afraid
To touch the ground;
Don't have to hear

Death rattle's sound.
Death comes as a shock;
It will never have to knock

Old man hides from death
Under his rock
But death takes him away anyway

Doesn't care
What he has to say
His life is now gone

Just faded away;
Too tangled up in his power;
He never expected death to call.

EPICS 3

Life is too short
To fight;
But sad man does it anyway

To flex his might;
Before he loses his sight;
He hides his eyes from the light

He was promised a chance
To expand his life;
Though the promise was broken;

Earth's water veins
Feel so much pain
Clogged and hardened

The light shines anyway
For it must
Nothing about trust

Light was made that way;
Mighty power;
To defy decay.

IV

I walked on the street
Going my way
I saw the mighty power

Lighting the way
It gave me life
And time to reflect

Why did I ever
Leave my love
In neglect.

I held on
So desperately
There was no door open to me

My tears got in the way
And I just could not see
My true love was waiting

And was so close to me
But everything was different
There were so many new streets

EPICS 3

That I did not know;
So many city lights
Shining too bright

The sky light
Was dimming
Even on the clearest of nights

I was too old now
To fight for my rights
I was still holding on

Desperately;
To the dream
That was so far out of sight,

I was losing my might
And I was losing my breath
I looked al around me

Property that I rented
But never would own
Been exploited all my life

But I never let my sadness show;
I played the game
So the thought police

S.E. McKENZIE

Would never know
For so much was so selected
And so much was neglected

I was holding on to the time left
Seeing the light reflected from the sky
Never having really lived

And not ready to die;
I held on once more
To a locked door;

The Ghetto Queen
Looked at me
With all the hate in her eyes

But I was still able to see
Through her disguise
Knowing if I had been wealthy

I would have never been so despised

I held on to the dream;
And could not let go
I walked on the

EPICS 3

And saw places
That I would never belong
I felt so weak

But I had to be strong.
I was going home;
Where my true love would be;

I was going home;
What was left of me;
I was going home;

While the light shone on my path;
I felt no fright
Though I knew death would come to me

In the darkness of night.
I lived in the shadow;
That is what I know

I feel the light all around me;
I can feel it glow;
I see all the love

That had never died;
I see all the love still living
So I knew

That the Nouveau Gestapo
Had been lying
To you.

V

I am the sun
I give power
To all;

Strong and weak
New-born
Or lost in decay;

I am the sun;
Power that keeps life so warm
I am the sun;
Where there is no hope left
I will be the one
To shine;

I am the sun.

THE END

CHAOS

S.E. McKENZIE

#39. CHAOS
I

Chaos; the ancient boss
When Hate and Fear
Are so near; calculate your loss;

In Chaos; the emptiness of Forever.

Forever
Good and Bad
A ladder to climb

Into the beast's mouth

There was so much doubt;
Free Speech
For one;

To incite;
To fight;
All night.

Fate;
The change of the state;
Lost in the hate;

Those without power;
To speak the truth;
Feared Forever

EPICS 3

The beastly mouth

Had taken over;
Now we must choose;
And still lose;

For the lesser of two evils;
A choice, not so great;
Feeds the fate of hate;

Anyway;
Could you stay
Awake?

For my sake;
Stay aware;
Of time;

The way; your fair share;
Of life is measured;
Will you stay

Until I understand
The line
That divides

But never multiplies?
Even when
A believer of True Love

Dies.

S.E. McKENZIE

I see Fear in the deer
I see Fear
In your eyes

The Force leaves no disguise
For the Collective
To criticize.

How the Collective pretends
That it bends;
For all; not just friends;

How the Collective hides when it takes;
And conceals its mistakes;
Name plates left in a pile; identity is never clear.

Blurred by Fear
And tear drops;
When the decay they made

Never stops growing;
Showing; behind the door;
Is a troll;

We run when we see him stroll.

So safe
In our tree
Are we.

EPICS 3

Though we cannot own our tree;
We
Are still free.

II

Predator
So willing to grant you a loan
Predator

Once in debt
You are partially owned
By another

Who will defy
When you ask
The truth

The Collective will lie;
So many stuck on the Pillory;
The watchers watch but cannot see;

As the Ghetto Queen
Laughs in glee;
The Nouveau Gestapo does not know

What he wants to be;
Used to be loved;
Now a stranger in a land

That he left behind.

S.E. McKENZIE

Now; choose the turning points.

How the debt grows
Into borrowed tomorrows
As the Collective

Roll in their greed;
Create so much need;
Refuse to let go of the deed;

As the Troll
Has no money
To pay for the toll

The new bridge
Was built
Without a fight

On foreclosed land
New demand
New command

He looks for his prey
Everyday
He throws so many away.

EPICS 3

Debtors insanity
Paves the way
As the Ghetto Queen laughs in glee.

The Troll
Looks for someone new
To balance his books

He looks; still stuck in a world so flat
And ready to oppose
Anyone who really knows.

How the grass grows
And how many on the other side
Stood their ground

As the Dinosaur lived Forever
In emulation
What a sensation

To build Forever;
A time no one knows how long
No reason to fight; just bask in the light

S.E. McKENZIE

Inside; now out; turning points
Climbing into the sky;
So little room left;

Turning; Forever;

Leaving nowhere for the next generation to roam;
So afraid were their Mommas
When they left their home

To stray into hostile lands.

So afraid
Of loss to order;
Strung along

Chaos on the surface
Has reason and rhyme
As you climb

Into the sky; Fear Forever.

THE END

//EPICS 3

PULSE

#40. PULSE
I

The Ghetto Queen
Expands her domain;
More for her to reign

Over; Never knowing Joe's name;
Her fear
Keeps Nouveau Gestapo near;

Cultural Genocide;
Destroying
The foundation inside;

Poison in a bottle;
Added to the mix;
Cultural Genocide; Economic Fix;

Her expertise
Cultural Genocide
She will put a label on you

Not caring if it is not true;
Now Joe has nowhere
To hide;

EPICS 3

For Ghetto Queen
Has destroyed
His pride;

Now filled with self-doubt;
Joe can only shout
Feels so ill; Ghetto Queen's thrill;

Cultural Genocide;
Wrong side
Of the wire

I feel it inside me;
Inside you;
Your Pulse is rising.

II

The Ghetto Queen's glare
The Battle Stare
She does not care

How she imposes'
Her devaluation of Joe and others;
Never treating them as sisters and brothers.

S.E. McKENZIE

Ghetto Queen can't play fair
For her Fear
Is owned

And the process
With no redress
Grabs cash fast.

Fear to buy
Fear to sell
Just another hell

For those
Who cannot tell
A foe from a friendly

The Battle Stare
Is always there
As she runs

Creating justification
And a new sensation
To trap those

EPICS 3

Who are sucked in
By her magnetic glare
Her Battle Stare.

Waves rise with the tide.
Where can Joe hide?
The Ghetto Queen's world is never wide

Still wild;
We watch those trapped trying to fight
Her Magnetic Force;

The war, just another power grab;

As she imposes
Her devaluation
On others;

Never treating them
As sisters or brothers;
As she destroys Joe's self-identity

He will crumble inside;
Weapon of war;
Guarded by Nouveau Gestapo

She darts outside her web of fear;
Her fear is always near
Ready to pounce and ruin the day;

As Fear's magnetic field surrounds Joe;
He has lost before he could begin;
No self-identity; Joe can't win;

The process
Was all about cash.
While Joe's mind is in a state of regress.

III
And love for the common man
Could not grow
In Ghetto Queen's heart.

She imposes
In mega doses
Rupturing self-identity of others

Never treating them
As sisters and brothers;
Imposed will; not goodwill;

EPICS 3

Seems like
Every generation
From before

Becomes Cannon Fodder
For those who rule;
Devalue others in a way so cruel

Just another tool for a fool;

While we lose ourselves in love;
Only the stars see the one
Fighting for his life

Lost in the storm
Just another boat wreck
No one wants to see

On their beach so fine
They don't have the time
To embrace Nature's rhyme.

IV
Just another Life
Pulsating; floating
Never able to stay

S.E. McKENZIE

Looking for a home
In the usual way
While the bulldozers

Ghetto Queen
Stares out her window
So alone

Her fear
Leads to the vision
Only she can assume

As she imposes

Predator Class; her mind
Full of suspicion
She makes a decision

Then toxifies
Poor man Joe's will to live;
Human Condition;

She pulls; the only way she can;
For the Ghetto Queen
Owns her fear; magnetic field;

EPICS 3

Her subject matter
Makes so many sadder
As she turns suspiciously

So many feel accused
And abused
Industry from Hell

Made
To buy
And sell

Ghetto Queen
Dirty fighter
Creates the dispossessed

Her social privilege and order
Can only make her
Fear more;

She locks the door;
Of her mind;
Becomes unkind;

S.E. McKENZIE

Baiting and hating
In a language of tongues
And forbidden to speak

Makes so many weak
But Nouveau Gestapo
Pretends to be strong;

With his hand on his gun
He holds it;
Until his fear is satisfied;

The Ghetto Queen
Assumed her bias;
just another member; predator class;

To her advantage;

Bury what they can
In the memory
Of yesterday;

Little magnets pull and push away;

Did you hear his cry
As Joe fought for his life
All alone on his boat?

EPICS 3

Joe tried to float;
Fighting the pull of the deep sea
Of fear and suspicion

That very one; with waves
Of overpowering pull;
Into Time and Infinity;

Lost in the sea;
Of uncertainty;
Now Joe's world is upside down

While Ghetto Queen glees behind her frown
How she loves
Putting Joe down.

Holding his life
Was about to capsize
Overloaded with fear and lies

Of yesterday
Joe could only know
What he had left behind;

His life so harsh;
He could not be kind;
His hunger made him blind;

S.E. McKENZIE

His hunger hurt so bad
He was about to lose his mind
While the Nouveau Gestapo

Stood by
While food was thrown away
He looked away

As the ghetto queen
Was wearing new attire
As she loved to hear.

V
Time heals;
Time kills;
And many kill time.

The beautiful voices
Sing in a Collective Choir
That Joe is excluded from;

He has his own song
With no one
To sing along.

EPICS 3

The ageing elite will soon tire
And fade away.
Into memories that will inspire;

So much glory
So much not said;
When repeating the story.

Creation

Destruction
Magnets attract
By opposite poles.

The poles clash
We like magnets are pulled
Into the magnetic field

Now stuck
We cannot be free
Until the pull weakens.

While Time heals;
Time kills
And many kill time.

S.E. McKENZIE

As the magnet pulls
There is nowhere to hide
From the force of Pull;

Power to buy and sell
Keeps us alive;
Expands possibilities;

Economies;
Feeding life
Difference between heaven and hell;

Who owns the means
Owns the story
Or so it seems

The beauty of the day
Takes my breath away;
And so quick to fade away

The moment cannot stay
But is now lost
In the emptiness

Of the past

EPICS 3

This side of life's beauty;
I see
Is astounding

Leaves my heart pounding

For I am alive
I will survive
To see another day

Just like today
Will fade way
Into tomorrow;

No one can see Joe;
All alone;
Clinging to what is left of his life;

Trapped in the magnetic pull;

Ghetto Queen's Battle Stare;
The Trumpet's Blare;
The Plague of Despair

So eager to share

S.E. McKENZIE

Famine, war, disease and hunger
Were never meant to be;
For Paradise

Was never meant to be
As cold as
Ghetto Queen's eyes;

Joe clung to life
In all his misery
He still wanted more;

His thirst for life
Was easy to ignore
While the Ghetto Queen

Closed her door.

THE END

EPICS 3

THE
DENOMINATOR

#41. THE DENOMINATOR

I

We go off to war
All of us
Together we are one;

Only numbers below the line.

We leave our homes and family
Hidden in mist
We hope we will be missed;

We fight
As we are told
We die before we grow old;

We are the numbers below the line.

Common denominator
That we all share; more than we dare;
Living below the line;

We ignore our fate;
We are shaped to hate
Whoever we are told

To hate; our hate
Makes us
Bold

EPICS 3

Before we die
Never too old;
Never showing

Our love-lights never glowing;

For we are too cold;
We have grown
Without ever knowing love;

We are just part of the flock;
Who we could have been;
Will stay unlocked;

Deep inside;
We learn to hide;
What we hope could have been.

For we live
Below the line;
All the time;

Only a few
Will get away
Alive; most of us will stay;

In this grave;
For as long as forever;
For we must stay

S.E. McKENZIE

Below the line.

Love has never been shown.
Love; the greatest value;
Always on loan;

For love
A greater force than you and I
A shadow we can only leave behind;

After we die;
We will grow
More loving and giving

After we die;
Part of we, will live in you;
Unconsciously; you know it is true;

Though the moment we die
No one will hear us cry;
We still wear our mask with pride;

Just a steely smile
Planted on our face; only place
Where we can hide.

EPICS 3

From it all
Before we fall
Off the wall

We must guard;
For evermore;
For He lives behind its door;

II

When was the beginning?
We will never know;
We are just part of the flock

Ruled by his clock;

To remind us that our time;
Belonged to others;
Owners; not brothers;

We hold on to the dream;
We pass it on
Before the last scream

We cling to our vision;
Before we let go;
Of the rest of our life;

S.E. McKENZIE

No crying we make;
We surrender to Eternity;
Which might just be

Another lie;
Maybe nowhere and nothing at all
Smaller than a spec on the wall;
That we guard before we fall.

III

We were told to never look back;
But I saw you looking back
Anyway;

Were you hoping
That the seed you had planted
Would have all your wished granted

So he could grow
Into tomorrow
Free from sorrow;

And remember you;
As the haunted ghost
Who loved him the most;

EPICS 3

For ever more
Behind a closed door;
People fight for their last breath

Before they walk in.

IV

To grow up in the usual way;
Maybe even better than that;
A world of peace;

While the arms' dealers
Turn a profit
We are left out in the cold

Never allowed to grow old;
And were never to be captured;
That is what we were told;

By a man
We would never know
Who lived in a tower

With a woman half his age;
Grew old fast with rage;
Would be replaced soon;

S.E. McKENZIE

Just like us;
We climb the wall;
For a moment we feel tall;

Before the fall;
For the man in the tower
Had it all

And still wanted more;

But we
Lived below the line;
Time after time;

Our seeds were left
To live for us
The way we could not;

We would soon be left
On this battle field to rot;
We left our seed to grow

A precious life
Into tomorrow
Burdened by our sorrow

One more cycle in a knot again

EPICS 3

Sometimes paralyzed in pain
Sometimes in love;
Soon to be swept into the heavens above

Or into the molten fire below;
We would never know;
If we could grow
A soul
Without having control
Over our fate

We try not to hate
He; who lives behind the door;
He who we guard

For evermore;

We grow into cycles
Spinning all around
One life ends

And one begins;
Bounded by time
Under the line.

THE END

S.E. McKENZIE

THE PULL

EPICS 3

#42. THE PULL
I

Sam was pulled
Like a puppet
On a string; rose above the tide;

As the wind came in.

Drowning in the beauty
Surrounding the wall, guarding it was his duty
To survive; to stay alive, he had to be a hero;

He grew from Love; magnetic force from above;
Opposing hate
To balance Mega-rich man's toxic state;

Favorite game of Bully-man;
Was to torment Sam;
Bully-man wanted Beauty; he wanted it all

Mega-rich Man's occupation and situation
Was built on a stack of cards;
He was protected by thousands of guards

Some are now resting in graveyards.
You are what you sew; even though
Bully-man was about to fall;

S.E. McKENZIE

False pride; envy in a land of plenty;
Never asking; always taking and faking;
Never knew if Mega-rich Man had lied.

Before he bought the massive wall;
For protection he said; the prison was in his head
Sam was never told;

The Gatekeeper from hell;
Would never tell
His true motivation;

When making a decision;
Offered help but then marked Sam like a beast
Big Boss; bigger Loss;

See how Mega-rich Man loves to feast;

Some pull;
Some push;
Not a word they speak;

Like a puppet on a string; holding on in the storm;
The dispossessed; victim of process;
Bully-men were always targeting the weak.

The Bully-men took it all;
Even though they are about to fall
After they finished building the wall.

EPICS 3

For Mega-rich Man

Wanted everything
That money could buy
To hear Beauty sing

And to listen to his lie;
He even owned Ghetto Queen's Dress;
For he controlled almost every material process.

All Sam could do was reflect
As he awoke from the night;
He wanted to do everything right;

But beauty was in his sight;
He was pulled by Beauty's might;
Nowhere to belong;

He had to stay strong
For he was just another hero
Guarding the wall.

There was no real redress;
For infinity had no door
For those without physicality.

Sam rose above the tide;
Water circling; no need to hide
Sam has never lied.

S.E. McKENZIE

Even though
Mega-rich Man
Tried to buy immortality

Immortality was just another lie.
What mattered
Was left behind

As Ghetto Queen put down her crown;
Without a word to speak;
How she praised the meek;

Needing something
To cling to; rising above the tides;
Conditions determine

Who Sam can be
Shaped by his drive to be free
Balanced by the moon and sun;

Holding on as the storm came in.

Out of bounds
Into a world
Beyond the wall

EPICS 3

The climb was hard; once on top
Sam felt so tall
Above the wall

But beneath the wall
Many were hoarding it all.
They were expecting the fall;

Never questioned where the wall
Would crumble;
For the watchers watched but could not see

Behind the wall
There was someone else's space;
There was another stranger's face.

Clinging on
While the storm raged;
The only event that wasn't staged.

II
False Pride; only feelings they say;
Pre-judged to feed greed; nothing you can do, they say;
Greed created so much need;

S.E. McKENZIE

Bully-man pushed into Sam
Sam was now possessed by Beauty;
Sneered as he apologized to Sam;

Smeared; as Bully-man lied;
Could not pull Sam's anger
From inside out

Or make Sam shout
Though Bully-man tried;
Grumpy old man beneath black hair dye;

Could never buy
Immortality
Though he tried; for he still believed the lie.

While Grumpy old man's anger grew;
For he knew;
His end would soon arrive;

He did all he could, and could not survive;
Once his hardened heart
Stopped pounding;

Would stay that way
For evermore;
In eternity; without a door

EPICS 3

For those without physicality;
To prepare;
One had to change one's mentality;

Bully-man picked on another;
Closed his ears
While Beauty cried;

Bully-man smirked
With pleasure;
Only power he ever knew;

He had nothing better to do.
Than to dominate with hate;
Toxified fate hose with less;

Bully-man said he had nothing to confess.

While the watchers watched but could not see;
How his heart was losing the flow;
Soon Bully-man would have to go;

Into infinity; chaotic;
No dialogue;
Disconnected

S.E. McKENZIE

Cannot relate
When in such a state
Could not hide

The power of his false pride
For evermore
For Infinity has no door

For those without physicality
There really is no
Immortality

It was all a lie
Though it was called truth;
As Bully-man's heart hardened

He hated anyone who still had youth.
And how his hate
Fed his fate while he ignored the truth;

For his greed
Kept so many in need;
Though he had no word

To speak out and shout.

He looked for the weak;
So he could pull out
Their anger to the surface

EPICS 3

And hear them shout
In desperation
Hurt sensation;

Just feelings pulled from the inside out;
What a game;
To make those behind the wall

Cry and shout out;
'We are dying and crying while you are lying,"
Nothing new at all.

III

As the big machines dig for oil and gas;
The owners and runners thought
The damage would pass;

How could the Earth not shake
During a man-made earthquake;
And how could the wall not fall?

It did, the wall came down
No longer a game;
For the wall could not stand;

Under false command
Even with a lot of guards
It was only built on a house of cards.

THE END

S.E. McKENZIE

CRACKER

#43. CRACKER
I

Cracker cracking his whip
He owns the ship
He is in charge of your life's trip;

Don't give him any lip;
And don't feel at ease
His Negativity is like a disease

So hard to please;
As he puts up the wall
He wants it all

And he carries the keys,
To your door;
Rebel against evil for evermore;

Rebel against Cracker's Negativity
That pushed you onto the floor;
His Negativity steals your time as he salivates;

He even owns your door.
Ghetto Queen with phone in hand
In her tight black jeans

S.E. McKENZIE

Is so quick to accuse,
Whoever walks behind;
Slams door in face with a look so unkind.

Nouveau Gestapo will beckon to her command.
We are not supposed to be seen
No one cares where we have been,

They have been indoctrinated,
And shaped by power of the lie,
How could they care if we cry?

Or what we know;
It is all about the show;
And the social media glow.

Dialectic of fear;
Taking over;
Acts like she owns every public place.

Addict of hate, Cracker salivates as he delegates;

Discriminates; loves to make others squirm;
Loves treating others
Worse than a worm.

EPICS 3

Impossible to please;
You will be begging
On your knees;

Everything fits to a T
He says "Look at the great me."
You will be crippled if you don't follow me.

Count the cost of your loss,
For Cracker is your cross boss.
No sweetness can grow in the Cracker's mind

For he is forever willfully blind;
Possessed by the product of being unkind
Processed when selling pain and degradation.

So quick to tear others apart; negative sensation;
His favorite sport is breaking your heart;
The Cracker is cruel, the Warhead his tool;

We are left behind,
Cracker would have it no other way;
He never listens to what others have to say.

The Cracker would own the air you breathe
If he only could;
Settles on breaking the minds

Of those beneath; in his social order;
He praises his new wall and himself;
Laughing in glee he says "hooray for me".

The Cracker demands that you give him
A submissive look
Because he is the one that has written the book.

To remember for eternity.
Know him to a T;
He will be watching you and me

He watches but cannot see
The people on the other side
Of the wall;

Not under his jurisdiction to control;
Though he will try
To buy their very soul.

II
The Warhead flew in the sky;
Over Cracker-town where everyone was getting by
The Warhead looked down on the pawns from the sky

As the Warhead cried out in pain;
"Don't wanna overkill
The underfed again.

EPICS 3

Don't want to kill
Little babies in the night
I want to hold on to you

And make love until the morning light
Shines in your hair;
Smile at me, show you care.

Don't want to be Cracker's delegate to instigate more hate;
Oh how I wish the Cracker could overcome
The hate in his heart; don't want to be a tool for a fool;

Or be made to me mindless and cruel;

Cracker made me tear apart people who had a heart;
I see Cracker celebrating instead of elevating those
Worse off than he; benefits the Cracker so easily."

III

Slum landlord, how he loves to discriminate;
The mass devaluation makes him salivate;
Doesn't value you enough to co-operate;

Blocks his ears when you try to communicate;
No need to elevate; nothing you say will he validate;
Won't fix the roof; teaches our young how to hate;

S.E. McKENZIE

Slum landlord won't fix anything at all
Slum Landlord is ghettoized too;
Will make you feel small and blue

As he lets all the paint peel
From the wall
The birds move into the hole in the hall.

Cracker addicted to negativity
He loves to salivate
When he preaches his Hate;

Cracker's followers
Are shaped with each word
Of indoctrination;

What a sensation.

They chirp so happily;
They never had it so good;
This is the way it is

When the Crackers
Own
The neighborhood.

They put up the wall;
So they don't have to see us at all;
And if they do; they feel new age rage;

EPICS 3

Lost conscience as they play
In the electronic
Killing field.

Everyone feels helpless; it is understood
Why evil pig farmer looked so good.
The wall grows higher every day;

So the gatekeepers to life
Have it all
Their way.

Cracker has engineered cruelty to a T
Always watching but cannot see
The value in me and you;

The opportunity cost;
What has been lost;
Behind the wall.

Trapped in Crackers assumption
A victim of his consumption;
Fall under his spell, you will lose your gumption

Cracker, addict of Negativity
That steals time from every day
Throwing his projection on you, his way.

S.E. McKENZIE

In our pad as cold as stone.
For the Cracker controls the thermostat.
Degradation hurt sensation; ancient frame of mind

To make Cracker glow in glee when being unkind;

Process of dehumanization; a hurt sensation;
Process creates the problem; Our life is shorter
Than his; he turns us against each other

No longer sister and brother;
Cracker addicted to Negativity
Takes control of the thermostat

Cracker tells you when to be warm
When to be cold;
How to live and how to grow old.

When we look up into the sky
We feel so alive
Which is better than wanting to die.

Cracker upsets the heart for sport;
While we fall through the cracks; faulty process;
No redress; Cracker's addiction to negativity

EPICS 3

Warps what is appropriate;
Makes him salivate
When he abuses power to discriminate.

Steals your life away.

Ghettoization
A new sensation
In this age that widens the gap

Between the haves and have nots
There is no cap;
Oh how the Cracker laugh

In the aftermath
As he grows richer; taking over
Without introduction;

Every day your value will be in reduction.

Sharing power
Is not what the Cracker will do;
He cracks the whip

With a sour face
And he soon will own
Everyplace.

S.E. McKENZIE

Your roof will leak
As you feel meek
He will yell at you

As you try to speak;
But the birds
Living in the hole in the hall

Have never had it so good;
That is what it is like
When the Crackers

Own the neighborhood.

Hear him fight
Over the hot water bill
That was so unfairly divided;

The Cracker way.
Building so high
Until there is no space in the sky.

IV

New age of rage;
Too young to die;
Too old to give it another try;

EPICS 3

Master class;
Smile
As you behave as a slave.

The Cracker will drive on by
The Revolving Door; before he comes to a stop;
He comes out and expects you to hop

At his bidding;
Refusing him is forbidden;
He carries a chain of keys;

To get along
You cannot speak
For Cracker will turn up the heat;

He is the master of the only reality now

He owns the doors
Of all the tenants in his block;
His callousness sends some into shock;

Poisoned and broken frame of mind;
Too hard to heal; the ghetto is now inside;
Now he is a victim of a world unkind;

So cruel when Cracker is willfully blind.

S.E. McKENZIE

Can't reflect just neglect one side;
Murdering the other side;
The ultimate sum zero game called war;

Kicking the living
Onto the floor; push them through
The Revolving Door; this power

And all its glory; couldn't be a more gory story;
Rewritten in misrepresentation;
As the Cracker's vibes caused a negative sensation;

As Cracker walks in without a knock;
He owns the block;
Don't like it

Then live under a rock.
For the Cracker does not have to be kind;
He can bully who he wants as he carries all the keys;

You work as a slave for nothing at all
For the building is about to fall;
The Crackers walk by

How they laugh
As they make you cry;
As we get buried in the aftermath.

EPICS 3

They don't even try
To communicate
To understand and to validate

Our value; Looks like a jailer
With all his keys;
He walks around proudly

He talks loudly;
About things that should have been private
Make him hate and salivate;

To get along
You must bow
Sometimes on your knees;

His Negativity
Spreads like a disease
Impossible to please;

You must hold on to the dream
Or your pain
Will make you scream

And to get along
You must not speak at all
Or be seen

S.E. McKENZIE

Unless you want
The Cracker to get mean.
See how he breaks another person's mind;

As the victim goes into shock;
The cracker doesn't have to knock;
For the Cracker owns the entire block.

New world order

Colder than ever before;
New age of rage
We are kicked

Until we fall on the floor
Now we know
What we were fighting for.

Did we bend over backwards to get along
As barriers were put up
No one wanted us to hang around.

In the crackers world they didn't want to see us at all;
That was why they put up the wall;
As we starved, too weak to crawl

The new religion
Was written on the dollar bill;
In God we trust

EPICS 3

While so much around us
Just turned to rust;
Poisoning the Earth's crust.

Disenfranchising
With a click of a phone;
Death sentence without a name;

We wondered about it all not knowing Cracker was to blame.
Did we bend over backwards enough
To get along?

Worked free like a slave;
And it still
Was not good enough.

Slandered by a click of the phone
By any mean girl who walks by
We are so hungry and cold

We could almost cry.

As Cracker slandered us
With self-fulfilling prophecies?
Did we bend over backwards enough?

What could have the world been
If it had more love?
As no entrance sign stunted progress for some

S.E. McKENZIE

The watchers turned away
For they could not see
On the other side of the wall.

Yes, we were up against the wall;
There was no empathy for us
At all.

Cracker did not want to see us;
Did not want to hear us;
Or live near us.

That is why he put up the wall.

We lived in one of the coldest countries on Earth;
Many of us turned to ice;
And were officially called missing;

No one wanted us in plain view;
No one spoke to us al
Or said "how do you do?"

They wanted us behind the wall.

We found places
Where grass
Could never grow.

We were circled
By strings of the unexplained;
Not knowing how much we had gained.

EPICS 3

As the Church Lady
And Grumpy Old Man
Yelled at us so rigidly;

Told us we were too stupid to understand
Had to follow their every command;
Or we would never know

How the real world works;
While Cracker had the keys;
We had our memories;

He turned the water
And Heat off;
And Church Lady said

Just close your eyes
And you will be saved
For soon you will be dead; lying in your grave.

And your Momma lacked skills";
The church lady shouted out loud
While the crowd turned around to stare

Church Lady said
That we did not know our own mind;
The new aggression;

S.E. McKENZIE

Negative suggestion;
Condescending
Without bending

Sell it as healing
Without a feeling;
Have us kneeling

With eyes closed in prayer
As if the crowd
Was not there;

How they laughed;
They did not care
Who we could have been

If the world had been fair.
We knew to not swallow their pill
Process of overkill the underfed;

That made others so ill and many dead
Just for Gestapo's thrill he said our pain
Was just in our head; Zombified

Part of them died while the church lady lied;
Some thought they had a friend to hold on to
In the end everyone turned away;

EPICS 3

Had nothing nice to say;
No one would answer the phone;
Left us all alone;

If we did not do exactly what they said;
Which would make our head
Dead;

Zombified; Hurt sensation;
Degradation;
State paid medication;

We were the sold out generation;
As the bulldozer surrounded
What was left.

Ready to pave the way
For a brand new
Super highway.

We were trying to figure out what to do
But everyone
Got in the way;

Gave us no say;
While Ghetto Queen
In her tight black jeans

S.E. McKENZIE

Gave us the usual look of hate;
Ask us if we were following her
Into town;

We did not know what to say
Too many negative emotions
Got in the way

Degradation;
Our hurt sensation
For were we the sold out generation.

As Church Lady sent the viscous rumor
By email; grew like a tumor
Soon all thought it was true;

And very few knew
Who we could have been
If given the chance;

Instead hate pierced our heart;
With one glance;
Tortured our mind;

While they looked
So willfully blind
They stomp as they dance;

EPICS 3

On your face;
Throw you
All over the place;

Church Lady thumped us
With her Holy Book;
She gave us her holier than though look.

While the bulldozer came to Cracker-town
Started knocking
Our affordable housing down;

Church lady tried to sell us a lie;
That we would be welcome
In a real home in the sky when we die.

And we could feel our alienation
A hurt sensation
In this world of so much degradation

Zombified by State Medication;
We tried to get along
So we didn't say a thing;

While the bulldozers
Crushed everything
That we had.

S.E. McKENZIE

Made us feel hopeless and bad;
The look on faces
Made us look mad.

And all could do
Was close our eyes in prayer
Wishing the world we knew

Was never there.

And then someone in the crowd
Screamed;
And we wish we had the life that our Momma had dreamed.

We knew the mob, so indoctrinated
Was being regulated; had been fed a lie
And that is why

They salivated as they hated;
The same lie that made us cry;
Sometimes made us want to die;

And made the Crackers rich.
The mass snob
Would be worse off than us.

When the string of the unexplained;
Brought chaos;
The real boss of loss.

EPICS 3

Though we knew our Momma
Tried her best to let us live in dignity;
It was the dawn of World War Three.

We rose up again in pain;
With new power
The Magnetic Field gave us

The unexplained string to hold;
Now we had more power
Than Cracker's hoards of gold.

The Magnetic Feld glowed around us;
As the new world's gate
Opened to us; free from hate;

In the old world; greed
Created need;
And Cracker took it all;

Manufactured pain and degradation to sell;
Without a purpose, he made hell;
As we watched it all burn;

How he used to scream at us;
Tell us to relearn
Now it was his turn;

S.E. McKENZIE

To feel the burn.

We had no time
To wait
For a turn;

Cracker told us to get along
Cracker told us we didn't belong
Cracker cracked his whip

Cracker demanded no lip;
Cracker did not need to be civil
For he owned it all

Happy to watch us crawl;
While he burned out our mind
With his slander so unkind;

Yes, in Cracker's world
There was nothing left for us
At all;

We were left
To die behind the wall
In one of the coldest lands on Earth;

EPICS 3

No one cared about our worth.
They told us to get along;
They told us that we did not belong.

And we felt the majestic
Power of the unexplained string
The chaos which grew in everything;

We hung on to it real tight;
We hung on to it with all our might;
We had so much love to give;

Though many said we had no right to live
We still had
Our love to give;

Though we could not communicate;
There was too much hate
Controlling fate;

As the wall shook
It came tumbling down;
All around.

THE END

Produced by S.E. McKenzie Productions
First Print Edition May 2016

Copyright © 2016 by S. E. McKenzie
All rights reserved.

Enquiries: 1(778)992-2453
Mailing Address:
S. E. McKenzie Productions
168 B 5th St.
Courtenay, BC
V9N 1J4

Email Address:
messidartha@aol.com

http://www.amazon.com/SarahMcKenzie/e/B00H9RWX48/

www.ingramcontent.com/pod-product-compliance
Lightning Source LLC
Chambersburg PA
CBHW060149050426
42446CB00013B/2732